Winning With The

Giuoco Piano

and the

Max Lange Attack

Andrew Soltis

Revised

2nd Edition

Chess Digest, Inc

ISBN: 0-87568-201-4

This is a revised and updated edition of "Winning with the Giuoco Piano and the Max Lange Attack — Soltis" (Chess Digest 1992). There are thirty revisions. Some so important in the Giuoco Piano that the author requested dropping *Winning With* from the title.

AUTHORS: Andrew Soltis
EDITOR: Ken Smith
COMPUTER TYPESETTING: Parley Long
COVER: Elaine Smith
PROOFREADER: Hugh Myers & Parley Long
FINAL PREPARATION & DIAGRAMS: Parley Long

PUBLISHER: Chess Digest, Inc.®, 1601 Tantor, (P.O. Box 59029) Dallas, Texas 75229

TABLE OF CONTENTS

INTRODUCTION 5

IS THE GIUOCO DEAD? 7

MEANWHILE, THE MAX LANGE..... 12

CHAPTER ONE 15
The Positional Giuoco and Other Alternatives
1 e4, e5 2 Nf3, Nc6 3 Bc4, Bc5 4 c3, Nf6 5 d4, exd
6 cxd4, Bb4ch
7 Bd2 21

CHAPTER TWO 32
Introduction — Moeller Attack
1 e4, e5 2 Nf3, Nc6 3 Bc4, Bc5 4 c3, Nf6 5 d4, exd
6 cxd4, Bb4ch
7 Nc3 32
7...Nxe4 8 0-0!, Bxc3 9 d5!
9...Ne5 37

CHAPTER THREE 44
The Old Main Moeller
9...Bf6 with 13...0-0 47

CHAPTER FOUR 56
The New Moeller (13...h6)
9...Bf6 with 13...h6 56

CHAPTER FIVE 73
Euwe's Strong Point Variation
1 e4, e5 2 Nf3, Nc6 3 Bc4, Bc5 4 c3
4...Qe7 73

CHAPTER SIX 82
Introduction — Max Lange
1 e4, e5 2 Nf3, Nc6 3 Bc4, Nf6
4 d4, exd4 5 0-0, Bc5 6 e5 83

CHAPTER SEVEN 91
Max Lange Main Line

CHAPTER EIGHT 100
The Anti-Max Lange Variation

CHAPTER NINE 112
Other Giuoco Defenses
1 e4, e5 2 Nf3, Nc6 3 Bc4
(a) The Hungarian Defense, 3...Be7 114
(b) Alekhine's Variation, 3...d6 118
(c) 3...g6 122
(d) 3...Qf6? 125
(e) 3...f5 126
(f) 3...Nd4 128

INTRODUCTION

As the tempo of tournament chess speeds up, the ranks of players are being divided into two opposing camps based on how they approach the opening.

One camp holds that in faster games, the priority should be on reaching a playable middlegame position as fast as possible — even if that risks a failure to obtain an edge for white or obtaining a small but clear disadvantage as Black. For example, the elastic series of hypermodern moves (1 Nf3, 2 g3, 3 Bg2, 4 0-0, and 5 d3/6 e4 or 5 b3/6 Bb2) is not likely to get you a plus-over-minus advantage. It's not likely to get you a plus-over-***anything*** against a player of about the same rating unless you're both beginners. But it won't get you the worst of it in the six or seven seconds it may take to play those moves.

The other school argues that chess is chess, regardless of the time control. This way of thinking maintains that you should always try to find the best move in a position. The most challenging move in the starting position is, by most accounts, 1 e4. The most resistant answer is, arguably, 1...e5.

The perfectionist approach then would require White to find a semi-forcing weapon that leads to complications most likely to lead to an advantage. After a century in which masters believe that weapon to be the Ruy Lopez, many amateurs search for something else. And one of the best places to look is at the Italian Game (2 Nf3, Nc6 3 Bc4). Whether Black risks the Giuoco Piano and its legendary Moeller Attack or directs play into the slightly more conservative lines of the Two Knights Defense, White can bring to the board an enormous arsenal of preparation.

By studying the key positions of this book — many of them analyzed out to the 25th move and beyond — you can begin a game quickly *and* enterprisingly. You'll have a lot more fun than after 1 Nf3, without sacrificing solidity.

Because it takes a good memory to play the Giuoco Piano and the Max Lange, you see these openings being played much more often in correspondence chess — when players have access to books — than in over-the-board chess. Be forewarned: if you don't like memorizing, these aren't the openings for you. But if you can master these lengthy variations, the rewards can be considerable.

IS THE GIUOCO DEAD?

One of the good reasons for playing these is that most opponents think they have been refuted long ago. There is a general suspicion that the Moeller Attack died before World War I. But then you see a game like the following, from the World Active Chess Championships:

Dzindzichashvili-Karpov, Mazatlan 1988 — **1 e4, e5 2 Nf3, Nc6 3 d4, exd4 4 Bc4, Bc5 5 c3, Nf6** (Rather than accept a Scotch Gambit pawn the former world champion would prefer to defend the Moeller Attack.) **6 cxd4, Bb4 ch 7 Nc3, Nxe4 8 0-0, Bxc3 9 d5, Ne5!? 10 bxc3, Nxc4 11 Qd4, 0-0 12 Qxe4**

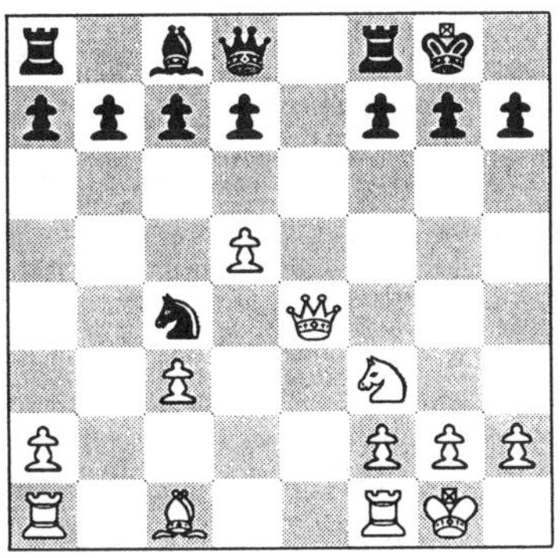

12...b5 13 a4, c6 14 axb5, cxd5 15 Qd4, Nb6 16 Be3, d6 17 Ra2, Be6 18 Re2, Nc4 19 Rfe1, Qd7 20 Qh4, Bg4 21 Qg3, Bxf3 22 Qxf3, Nxe3 23 Rxe3, Qxb5 24 Re7, a5 25 h4, a4 26 Rc7, Rae8 27 Rxe8, Qxe8 28 Ra7, h6 29 g3, Qe4 30 Qxe4, dxe4 31 Rxa4, Rc8 32 Rd4, Rc6 33 c4, f5 34 h5 and the game ended in a draw.

That's right, former world champion Karpov was outplayed in the opening — in a Moeller Attack.

Perhaps we regard the Giuoco as out of date because it has such a long history. It was analyzed by most of the great pre-1800 players and resulted in some of the great victories of the 19th century. Towards the end of that century it fell from favor. As Henry Bird wrote in the 1880's: " This opening is not quite so much in favor with the leading players as it formerly was. It is considered the lead to a somewhat dull form of game, and a few years since quite a prejudice arose in certain chess circles against it." Still, it could produce sparkling chess. One of the first brilliancy prize winners ever awarded was this:

Schiffers-Harmonist, Frankfurt 1887 — **1 e4, e5 2 Nf3, Nc6 3 Bc4, Bc5 4 c3, Nf6 5 d4, exd4 6 cxd4, Bb4 ch 7 Bd2, Bxd2ch 8 Nbxd2, d5 9 exd5, Nxd5 10 Qb3, Nce7 11 0-0, 0-0 12 Rfe1, c6 13 a4, Qc7 14 Rac1, Nf4 15 Ng5, Neg6**

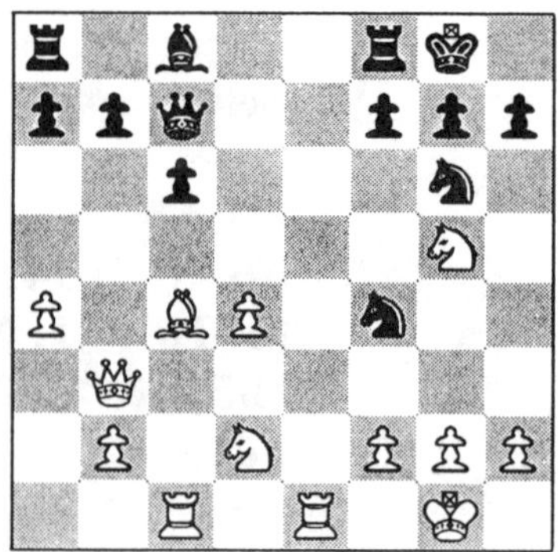

16 Re8!, Rxe8? (16...Be6!) **17 Bxf7 ch, Kh8 18 Bxe8, Ne2 ch? 19 Kh1, Nxc1 20 Nf7 ch, Kg8 21 Nh6 ch, Kf8 22 Qg8 ch, Ke7 23 Bxg6, hxg6 24 Qxg7 ch, Kd8 25 Qf8 ch, Kd7 26 Ne4!, Qd8 27 Qd6 ch, Ke8 28 Nf6 ch Resigns**

What breathed new life into the Giuoco was the replacement of the "positional" **7 Bd2** with the gambiting **7 Nc3!**. The latter move had been played a few times before the turn of the century but not really tested. In fact, when **7 Nc3** was played by Daniel Harrwitz in a famous 1846 match with Howard Staunton, Staunton didn't play the obvious **7...Nxe4** but the timid **7...d6** — and yet after **8 h3?!, h6 9 0-0, 0-0 10 Bb3, Ne7** won a strange game as Black.

It was Wilhelm Steinitz, in his "The Modern Chess Instructor," and later in his celebrated victory over Bardeleben at Hastings 1895 that made the Giuoco modern. And it was the discovery of Jorgen Moeller's move, **9 d5!**, (after 7 Nc3, Nxe4 8 0-0, Bxc3) that increased White's chances significantly.

Here is another brilliancy prize game, but from a later era than Schiffers-Harmonist. Note the move order, which seems to start out as a Center Game, then a Scotch, then perhaps a Max Lange and finally transposes into a Moeller.

Lazard-Gibaud, Paris 1909 — **1 e4, e5 2 d4, exd4 3 Nf3, Nc6 4 Bc4, Bc5 5 c3, Nf6 6 cxd4, Bb4 ch 7 Nc3, Nxe4 8 0-0, Bxc3 9 d5, Bf6 10 Re1, Ne7 11 Rxe4, d6 12 g4!?, h6 13 h4, Kf8 14 h5, g5 15 Nd4, c6 16 Qf3!, Nxd5 17 Bd2, Nc7? 18 Rae1, d5**

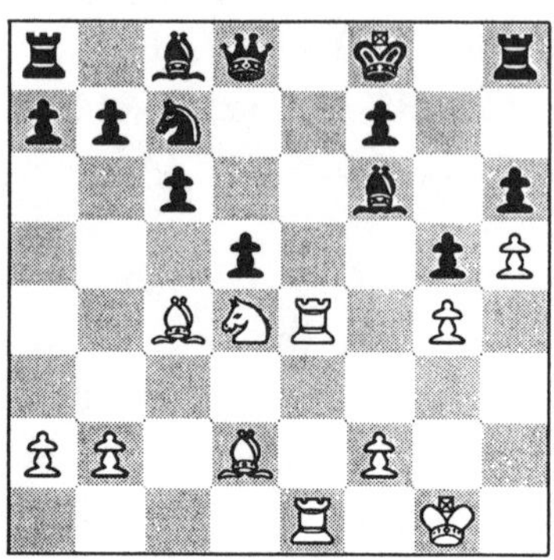

19 Bb4 ch!, Kg7 20 Re7!, dxc4 21 Nxc6, Qd3 (21...bxc6 22 Qxf6 ch!, Kxf6 23 Bc3 mates) 22 **Rxf7 ch!!, Kxf7 23 Re7 ch!, Kg8 24 Qxf6, Rh7 25 Re8 ch! Resigns**

In more recent times, the Moeller Attack has been a favorite of Paul Keres, whose analysis indicated White could not achieve more than a draw. Worse news came in 1969 when Lajos Portisch found a powerful new defense by Black that appeared to refute the Moeller. But, as chapter three and four will show, reports of the Giuoco's demise have been greatly exaggerated.

Nyffeler-A. Kovacs, Correspondence 1989-91 —
1 e4, e5 2 Nf3, Nc6 3 d4, exd4 4 Bc4, Bc5 5 c3 (a painless transposition into the Moeller), **Nf6 6 cxd4, Bb4 ch 7 Nc3, Nxe4 8 0-0, Bxc3 9 d5, Bf6 10 Re1, Ne7 11 Rxe4, d6 12 Bg5, Bxg5 13 Nxg5, h6!? 14 Qe2!, hxg5 15 Re1, Be6! 16 dxe6, f6 17 Re3!, d5 18 Rh3, Rxh3 19 gxh3, g6 20 Qf3, Qd6!? 21 Qxf6, Qf4.**

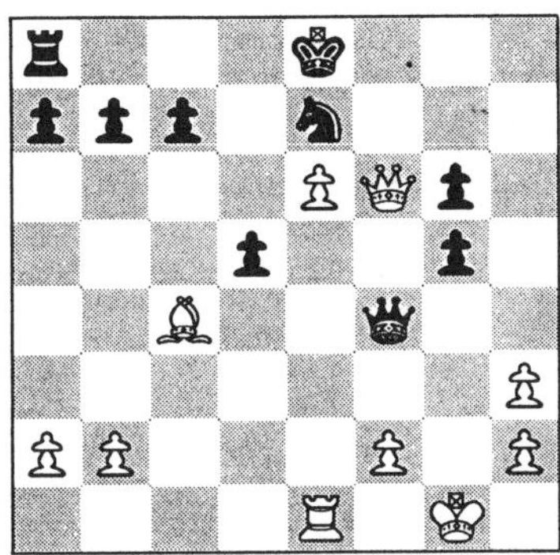

Better than 21...0-0-0 22 Bd3 which appears to favor White. Now the endgame should be excellent for Black after 22 Qxf4?. So White tried for more than the equality of 22 Qh8 ch, Qf8 23 Qd4, Qf4 and played **22 Qh8 ch, Qf8 23 Qxf8 ch, Kxf8 24 Bd3, Kg7 25 Kg2** and nearly had a winning position after **25...Rd8 26 Kg3, Rd6 27 Kg4, Kf6 28 Re3, Rxe6? 29 Rxe6 ch, Kxe6 30 Kxg5, c5 31 f4!**.

Later misplay led only to a draw (31...c4 32 Bxg6, Nxg6 33 Kxg6, Ke7 34 Kf5??, d4 35 Ke4, d3 36 Ke3).

MEANWHILE, THE MAX LANGE.....

The Max Lange attack perfectly complements the Moeller Attack. It provides White with a trappy method of complicating Black's life if he plays the Two Knights Defense **3...Nf6** instead of **3...Bc5**. Probably no other opening gives the Black player so many ways to lose quickly as the Max Lange. A typical example:

Kazic-Vukovic, Yugoslavia 1940 —
1 e4, e5 2 Nf3, Nc6 3 Bc4, Nf6 4 d4, exd4 5 0-0, Bc5 6 e5, d5 7 exf6, dxc4 8 Re1 ch, Kf8? 9 Bg5!, gxf6 10 Bh6 ch, Kg8 11 Nc3!, Bg4 12 Ne4, Bd6 13 c3, Ne5?

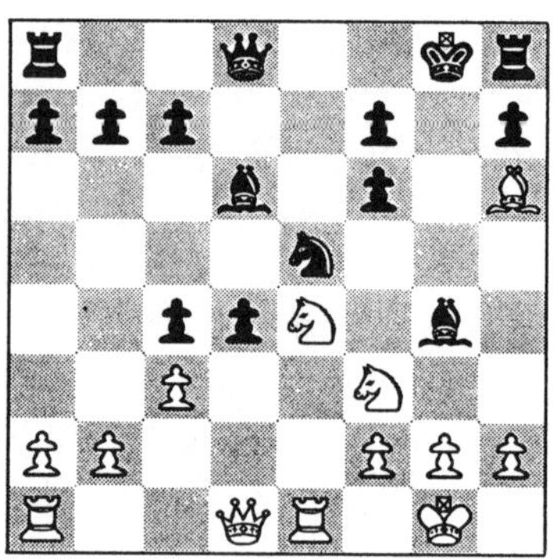

14 Nxe5!, Bxd1 15 Nd7!, Be7 16 Nexf6 ch, Bxf6 17 Re8 ch, Qxe8 18 Nxf6 mate.

Just before World War I the Max Lange fell into disrepute, as it appeared that once Black avoids all the little traps, he should stand better. However, the Max Lange got a powerful boost by

Frank Marshall's victory with it over Siegbert Tarrasch at Hamburg 1910.

Ever since then there have been doubts about Black's real survival chances. In fact, most grandmasters will avoid the opening entirely by playing **5...Nxe4**. However, as shown in chapter eight, White has good winning chances there too.

The key to evaluating **5...Nxe4** appears to depend on what happens after **6 Re1, d5 7 Bxd5, Qxd5 8 Nc3, Qa5 9 Nxe4, Be6 10 Neg5, 0-0-0 11 Nxe6, fxe6 12 Rxe6, Bd6 13 Bg5, Rde8 14 Qe1!, Qxe1 ch 15 Raxe1, Rxe6 16 Rxe6, Kd7 17 Re4, Re8 18 Rxe8, Kxe8.**

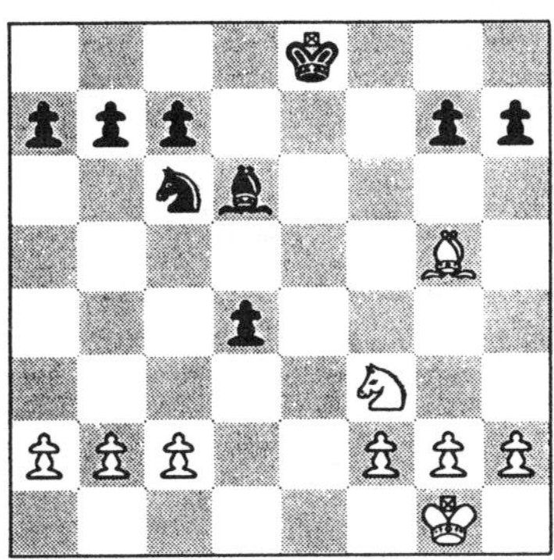

This endgame, the almost-inevitable result of 14 Qe1, had been considered — if anything — favorable to Black. But since the first version of this book appeared in 1992 opinion has been altered sharply. It accounted for a 300-point underdog upsetting endgame connoisseur Arthur Bisguier at the 1995 U. S. Open. The game, J. Ahmed-GM Bisguier, continued:

19 Kf1, Kd7 20 Bd2, h6 21 Ke2, Ke6 22 Kd3, Kd5 23 Nxd4! and Black, who saw the futility of 23...Nxd4 24 c4 ch, Ke5 25 f4 ch, as analyzed in chapter eight, tried **23...Ne5 ch 24 Kc3, Ng4** after which the game became confused (25 Be3?, Nxh2 26 Kd3, Ng4 27 c4 ch, Ke5 28 Nf3 ch, Ke6 29 Bd4, Bf8 30 Nd2, c5? 31 Be3, g6 32 f3, Nxe3 33 Kxe3, Bg7 34 Ne4, b6 and White won the good-N-versus-bad-B battle after 35 b3, Bb2 36 f4, Bd4 ch 37 Kf3, a6 38 a4, h5 39 g4, a5 40 Ng3, h4 41 Nf1, Kf6 42 Nd2, etc.).

Our survey of these two openings looks like this:

Chapter One: The Positional Giuoco and Other Alternatives

Chapter Two: Moeller Attack — Introduction

Chapter Three: The Old Main Moeller

Chapter Four: The New Moeller (13...h6)

Chapter Five: Euwe's Strong Point (4...Qe7) Variation

Chapter Six: Introduction to the Max Lange

Chapter Seven: Max Lange Main Line

Chapter Eight: The Anti-Lange Variation (5...Nxe4)

Chapter Nine: Other Giuoco Defenses

One final tip before we get started — The name is pronounced *"Joke-O"*......

Chapter One

THE POSITIONAL GIUOCO AND OTHER ALTERNATIVES

This section is by way of introducing the reader to the preliminaries of the Giuoco Piano main line and also to offer a few ways of conducting the middlegame without having to memorize pages of Moeller Attack analysis. One of these alternatives, the quiet **7 Bd2**, will be considered in greater depth than the others.

1	**e4**	**e5**
2	**Nf3**	**Nc6**
3	**Bc4**	**Bc5**

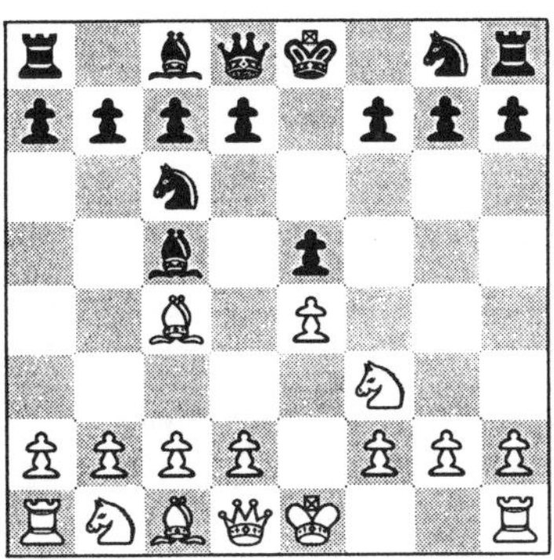

4 c3

If you really want to get your opponent out of the books, then **4 Nc3, Nf6 5 Nd5!** is the best try. You are then playing a position that occurs in the Rubinstein Variation of the Four

Knights Defense with colors reversed (1 e4, e5 2 Nf3, Nc6 3 Nc3, Nf6 4 Bb5, Nd4 5 Bc4, Bc5!).

Virtually the only recent analysis of this rare line appeared in the Soviet weekly "64" during the 1970's by I. Glazkov. He showed that **5...d6** allows a strong **6 d4!, Nxd4 7 Nxd4, Bxd4 8 Bg5** (8...Bxf2 ch 9 Kf1!, c6 10 Nxf6 ch, gxf6 11 Qf3!) or **7...Nxd5 8 Bb5 ch!?, Kf8 9 Nb3, Bb4 ch 10 c3, Nxc3 11 bxc3, Bxc3 ch 12 Bd2, Bxa1 13 Qxa1** with advantage to White.

And if Black accepts the gambit with **5...Nxe4 6 Qe2** he then gets into immediate trouble:

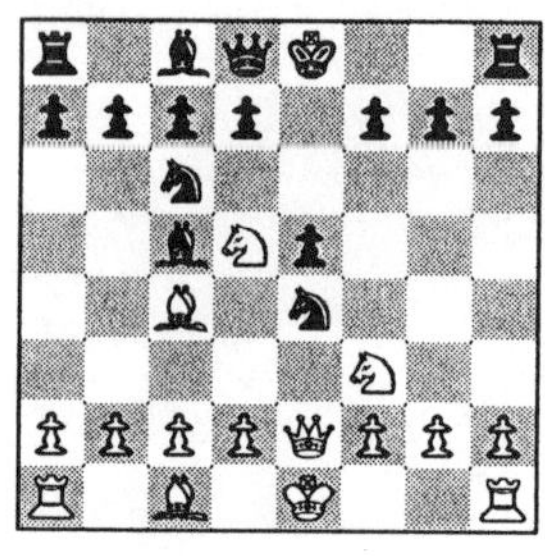

(a) **6...Nxf2 7 d4!**, wins material;

(b) **6...Bxf2 ch 7 Kd1** and **8 d3**, ditto;

(c) **6...Nd6 7 d4, Nxd4** (7...Bxd4 8 Nxd4, Nxd4 9 Qxe5 ch, Ne6 10 Bd3, 0-0 11 Be3, Ne8 12 0-0 with great development) and now **8 Nxd4, Bxd4 9 c3** is fine and **8 Qxe5 ch, Ne6 9 Bd3, 0-0 10 b4!, Bb6 11 Bb2, Ne8 12 Qh5, g6 13 Qh6, c6 14 h4!** is better;

(d) **6...Nf6 7 d4, Nxd5** (White is to be favored after 7...Bxd4 8 Bg5!, d6 9 c3, Bb6 10 Nd2 followed by Ne4, or 7...Nxd4 8 Qxe5 ch, Ne6 9 Bg5, Be7 10 Nxe7, Qxe7 11 0-0-0, d6 12 Qe3, 0-0 13 Nd4 and Nf5) **8 dxc5!, Nf6 9 Nxe5, 0-0 10 0-0, d5 11 cxd6, cxd6 12 Nxc6, bxc6 13 Bg5** with advantage to White thanks to the pinning bishop.

4 ... Nf6

Much too passive is **4...d6** because of **5 d4** when **5...exd4 6 cxd4, Bb4 ch 7 Nc3** gives White all the advantages of a Moeller Attack (better center, lead in development) but at none of the risk. See also the note to Black's sixth move below.

5 d4 exd4

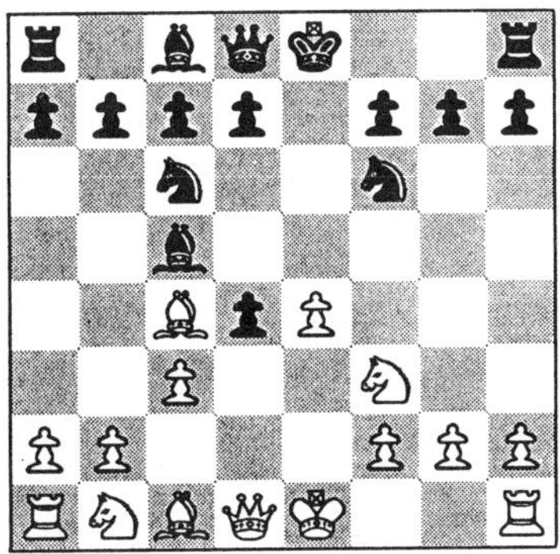

Periodically, some attempt is made in amateur or correspondence play to revive the gambit **6 0-0!?**. Acceptance is risky as shown by Stein-Langeweg, Plovdiv 1983 — a fairly recent game that mirrored 19th century theory: **6...Nxe4 7 cxd4, Be7?! 8 d5!, Nb8 9 Re1, Nd6** (9...Nf6 10 d6!) **10 Bd3, 0-0 11 Nc3, Ne8? 12 d6!!, cxd6 13 Bxh7 ch!, Kxh7 14 Rxe7, Qxe7 15 Nd5** and Black resigned in view of **15...Qd8 16 Ng5 ch, Kg6 17 Qg4, f5 18 Qh4** followed by **Qh7 ch.**

An indication of the age of this line is the comment that Black's 12th move was a rare deviation from **12...Nxd6 13 Bf4, Ne8** and now White again wins with **14 Bxh7 ch!, Kxh7**

15 Rxe7!, Qxe7 16 Nd5, Qd8 17 Ng5 ch, Kg6 18 Qd3 ch, f5 19 Qg3 as in Homezen-Brady, 1897.

And there was also the earlier example of this same trappy line in Neumann-Guretsky — Cornitz, match 1863, in which White varied with **10 Bb3** instead of **10 Bd3** and won even faster: **10...0-0 11 Nc3, Ne8 12 d6!, cxd6 13 Rxe7, Qxe7 14 Bg5, Nf6 15 Nd5, Qd8 16 Qd4, Nc6 17 Qh4** Resigns!.

And if, instead of accepting the gambit, Black continues meekly with **6...d6 7 cxd4, Bb6**, as some analysts have recommended, then we transpose into a favorable position for White that is usually reached via **6 cxd4, Bb6?! 7 0-0**. (See note to the main line 6...Bb4ch.)

Further if, after **6 0-0**, Black rejects the offer with **6...d3**, White appears to have good chances with **7 b4, Bb6?! 8 a4, a6 9 e5, d5 10 Bxd3, Ne4 11 Qc2, Bf5 12 Ba3** as in a Soviet correspondence game, Estrin-Korelov, or (in the above) **8 e5, d5 9 Bxd3, Nd7 10 Bg5, Ne7 11 c4, dxc4 12 Bxc4, 0-0 13 e6!** (Polyantsev-Bass, USSR 1974).

The **6 0-0** gambit is important because it can occur in different move orders (e.g. a Max Lange-ish 1 e4, e5 2 Nf3, Nc6 3 Bc4, Nf6 4 d4, exd4 5 0-0, Bc5 and now instead of 6 e5 there is 6 c3!?, transposing into our gambit). The crucial line is **6...Nxe4 7 cxd4, d5!**. White can obtain compensation only in the endgame with **8 dxc5, dxc4 9 Qxd8 ch** (not 9 Qe2, Qd3!). The outlook then is unclear:

(a) **9...Nxd8 10 Re1, f5 11 Nc3, 0-0 12 Nxe4, fxe4 13 Rxe4, Be6 14 Nd4, Bd5 15 Re5** and later **Nf5-d6** won for White in Popov-Schneider, Correspondence Olympiad 1975.

(b) **9...Kxd8! 10 Rd1 ch, Bd7 11 Be3, Kc8** (Also playable is 11...Ke7 12 Na3, Be6 but not 11...b5? 12 a4!, b4 13 Nd4 with a nice game.) **12 Rc1, Be6 13 Na3, c3! 14 bxc3, b6 15 Nd4, Bd7** and Black won in Kopylov-Govbinder, USSR Correspondence Championship 1975-6. White can improve a bit with **11 Ng5, Nxg5 12 Bxg5 ch, f6 13 Bf4** and Na3 but it doesn't appear to offer more than equality.

6 cxd4

Besides **6 0-0** and the text move there is another, potentially important line and that is **6 b4!?** with the idea of driving Black's knight off c6 with **7 b5**.

For example, **6 b4, Bb6 7 e5, d5** (Supposedly favorable to Black.) was tested in Romero Holmes-Estremera, Leon 1989 and was found to favor White after **8 exf6, dxc4 9 b5!, Na5 10 Qe2 ch, Be6 11 fxg7, Rg8 12 Nxd4, Bxd4? 13 cxd4, Qxd4 14 Bb2, Qd3 15 Bf6!**.

Similarly, on **6...Be7** White continues **7 b5, Na5 8 Bd3** with a promising initiative after **8...dxc3 9 e5**, e.g. **9...Ng8? 10 0-0, d5 11 Nxc3, c5 12 Qc2, g6 13 Rd1, Be6 14 Qa4** as in Romero Holmes-Weldon, New York 1988.

6 ... Bb4 ch

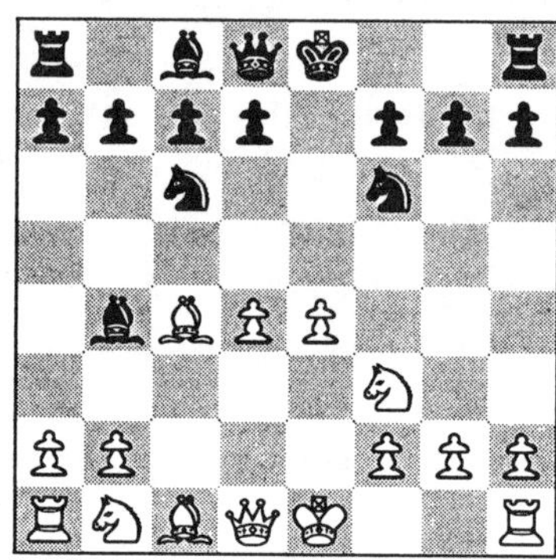

If Black fails to gain time with this check, White will have achieved a model center without cost. In a once-popular line of the Evans Gambit (4 b4, Bxb4 5 c3, Ba5 6 d4, d6 7 0-0, exd4 8 cxd4, Bb6) White has to surrender a pawn to get the same thing. Here **6...Bb6** leaves White with a free hand and he can obtain an edge with the simple **7 0-0** or the more forceful **7 d5**.

At one time **7 0-0, d6** was considered relatively safe for Black, because of his counter-pressure on the center, as in **8 Nc3, Bg4 9 Be3, Qe7**. But then White can continue **10 h3, Bxf3 11 gxf3, 0-0-0** (Johner-Tartakower, Baden 1914) and now **12 a4!** with a strong queenside chances and a solid center.

White can probably do even better with **7 d5**. Then there could follow **7...Ne7 8 e5** (e.g. 8...Ng4 9 d6!, Bxf2 ch 10 Kf1, cxd6 11 exd6, Nf5 12 Qd3, g6 13 Qe4 ch or 9...Nxf2 10 Qb3, Nxh1 11 Bxf7 ch, Kf8 12 Bg5! or 9...cxd6 10 exd6, Nf5 11 Qe2 ch and 12 Qe4!).

Note that on **7 d5** Black cannot shift his knight to a5

because **8 Bd3** will win a piece with a subsequent b2-b4!. This is a recurring idea that will create problems for Black if White gets to advance his d-pawn in other variations.

7 Bd2

With this move White exchanges pieces and seeks the contentment of a middlegame in which he has better pawn control of the center — particularly with the c5 and e5 outposts — than his opponent. The books do not regard **7 Bd2** as sufficient for more than equality but it has been successfully played by some prominent grandmasters (e.g. Tony Miles, John van der Wiel, Yevgeny Sveshnikov) for years.

More aggressive players — and those who like to reel off heavy analysis against unsuspecting foes — will prefer the Moeller Attack (chapters Two-Four).

7 ... Bxd2 ch

The immediate **7...d5 8 exd5, Nxd5** is faulty because **9 Bxb4!, Ncxb4** (9...Ndxb4 10 d5) misplaces a Black knight. White then creates tactical problems with **10 Qb3!** followed by **11 a3**, e.g. **10...Qe7 ch 11 Kf1, Nb6 12 Bxf7 ch** (12...Q-xf7 13 Qxb4; 12...Kf8 13 Ne5).

Note that **7...d5 8 exd5, Bxd2 ch** does not transpose into our main line below if White know enough to play **9 Qxd2!**, since he can then develop his QN more aggressively (9...Nxd5 10 0-0, 0-0 11 Nc3!, N6e7 12 Rfe1 with an obviously freer game for White than in our main line.

There is, however, a slightly more playable alternative to **7...Bxd2 ch** and it lies in **7...Nxe4** (Compare this with the note to Black's next move.)

After **7...Nxe4 8 Bxb4, Nxb4** White regains his pawn tactically with **9 Bxf7 ch!, Kxf7 10 Qb3 ch, d5** and now **11 Qxb4** and **11 Ne5 ch!?** should both give White a slight edge — as Greco had figured out before 1620. The simplest way to get an edge is **11 Qxb4, Re8 12 0-0** and now on **12...c6**, as played in a Zukertort-Steinitz match game way back in 1872, Steinitz's improvement of **13 Nbd2!, Nf6 14 Rae1, Qb6 15 Qc3** does the trick. White has the free use of the e5 outpost and that counts here.

8 Nbxd2

Here, of course, White must retake with the knight because 8 Qxd2 loses the e-pawn.

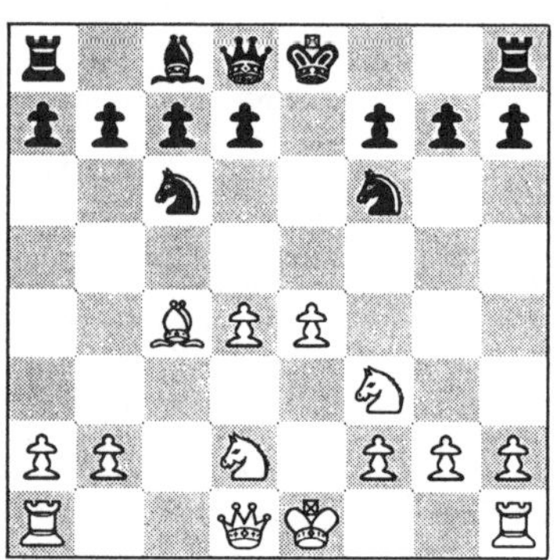

8 ... d5

In the first round of the 1963-64 U.S. Championship Edmar Mednis tried this opening as White and was mildly surprised when Bobby Fischer responded with the discredited **8...Nxe4!?**. What Bobby had in mind against the "book refutation" — **9 d5!, Nxd2 10 Qxd2, Ne7 11 d6!** and now **11...cxd6 12 0-0-0** or **12 Qxd6** — is not known. And, until Bobby comes back to the board, it will probably remain that way.

The methodical Mednis preferred **9 Nxe4, d5 10 Qe2** (Not 10 Bxd5, Qxd5 11 Nc3, Qe6 ch.) and insured himself of a slight edge due to his advantage in space: **10...0-0 11 0-0-0, Bg4 12 h3, Bxf3 13 gxf3, dxc4 14 Qxc4, Qh4 15 Kb1.**

9 exd5 Nxd5

The lines for the middlegame are drawn: Black will have an isolated pawn to batter and the fine control of d5 as an outpost. White will have pressure along the c4-f7 diagonal and the queenside files, as well as his own outpost at e5. Theory regards White as needing immediate activity to prevent the game from slipping into a drawish endgame, e.g. **10 0-0, 0-0 11 Re1, Bf5 12 Ne4** — a series of plausible but uninspired moves by — White led to a quick handshake in Tartakower-Gruenfeld, Baden Baden 1925 after **12...Bxe4! 13 Rxe4, Qd6 14 Qd2, Rad8 15 Rae1, Nf6 16 Re6, Qb4!**.

However, the likely endgames are not so even as we'll see, and White has ways of improving the position if Black stays in the middlegame.

10 Qb3!

This is now regarded as the only attempt at more than equality. There are, however, some modest methods of playing the middlegame that offer more than a draw. For example, **10 0-0, 0-0 11 Nb3** eyes the c5 square as an outpost. After **11...b6 12 Ne5, Bb7** White centralizes with **13 Qf3, Nce7**

14 Rfe1, Qd6 15 a3, Rad8 16 Nd2 and **17 Ne4** as in Yermolinsky-Krasenkov, Pinsk 1986.

White's advantage grew slowly: **16...Ba8 17 Ne4, Qh6 18 Rad1, Ng6 19 g3!, Nxe5 20 dxe5, Qg6 21 h4!, Ne7** and then **22 h5!, Rxd1 23 Rxd1, Bxe4** (23...Qxe4? 24 Qxf7 ch! and mate) **24 hxg6, Bxf3 25 gxf7 ch, Kh8 26 Rd7** built a winning endgame.

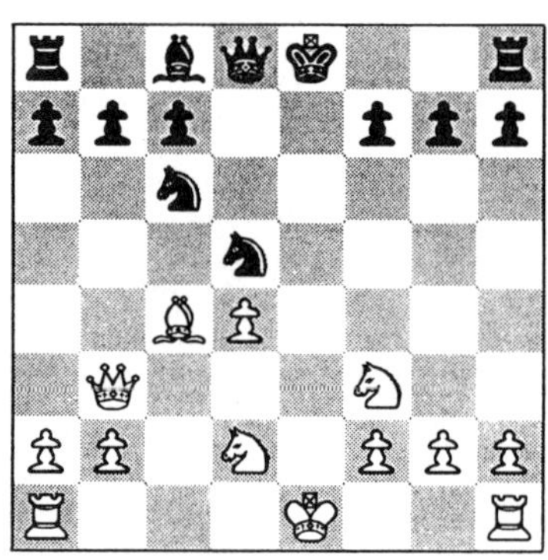

10 ... Nce7

There are two clearly inferior alternatives here and a third which is a none-too-discreet offer of a draw:

(a) **10...0-0 11 Bxd5, Na5** regains the sacrificed piece but **12 Bxf7 ch, Rxf7 13 Qc3** wins a pawn without serious compensation for Black;

(b) **10...Be6 11 Qxb7, Na5** is another pawn sacrifice that here is unsound because of **12 Bb5 ch!** (12...Kf8 13 Qa6, c6 14 Ba4). This checking possibility, incidentally, explains why 10 Qb3 is better than **10 0-0, 0-0 11 Qb3.**

(c) **10...Na5** used to be played in the 19th century with the continuation of **11 Qa4 ch, c6**. This, however, leaves the Black knight in limbo and after **12 Bxd5!, Qxd5 13 0-0** (or 13 Rc1 threatening 14 b4) White retains his initiative for several moves, e.g. **13...0-0 14 Rfe1** or **13...Be6 14 Rac1**.

However, there is a simple finesse in this last line that wasn't appreciated until the 20th Century when a draw was seen as a minor victory for Black. Instead of pushing a pawn at move 11, Black can play **11...Nc6!**, inviting White to repeat the position with **12 Qb3, Na5 13 Qa4, Nc6**. This, in fact, has become a notorious "GM draw" variation, as in the 13-move game Short-Karpov, Skelleftea 1989.

Therefore, White needs an improvement after **10...Na5 11 Qa4 ch, Nc6**. It won't lie in the natural **12 Ne5, 0-0 13 Nxc6** because of **13...Qe8 ch!** (14 Kd1, Nb6 with advantage to Black).

The Soviet GM Yevgeny Sveshnikov has tried **12 Bb5** with the idea of **12...0-0 13 Bxc6, bxc6** and now not **14 Qxc6, Re8** with compensation but **14 0-0!**. However, Sveshnikov-Mortensen, Leningrad 1984 went **12 Bb5, Bd7 13 Qb3?!, Qe7 ch 14 Kf1, Be6!** and Black had assumed the initiative (15 Bxc6 ch, bxc6 16 Qc2, 0-0 17 Qxc6, Nb4). White must try something like 13 0-0, 0-0 14 Rfe1 or 14 Qb3 if he wants to get something out of the opening. For example, **14 Rfe1, a6 15 Bf1!, Ncb4 16 Qb3, Bf5 17 Rac1** and in Morssink-van Bil, Correspondence 1990 White gradually took over the queenside (17...a5 18 a3, a4 19 Qc4, Nc6 20 Qb5, Bc8 21 Ne4, Ra5 22 Qd3, Bf5 23 Qd2 and Nc5).

11 0-0 0-0
12 Rfe1

Simple chess: the rooks will go to e1 and either c1 or d1. White is all ready now to double on the e-file: **12...Rb8?! 13 Re5!, Be6 14 Ng5, Nc6 15 Nxe6** and **16 Re4** with advantage (Voelkl-Rabidu, Correspondence 1980-81).

The chief alternative is **12 Ne5** after which **12...c6,** reinforcing d5, is often played. Then **13 Ne4** is a natural way of continuing. In Miles-Korchnoi, South Africa 1979 Black offered a trade of queens with **13...Qb6** with the usual endgame after **14 Rad1, Qxb3 15 Bxb3, Rd8 16 Rfe1, Kf8 17 f3, f6.** White still stands a bit better but it turned out badly for him when he chose a misguided plan of advancing his g-pawn. See Illustrative Game (1).

Another way of playing after **12 Ne5, c6 is 13 a4, Qb6** with play similar to the main line below (14 Qxb6, axb6 15 Bxd5, Nxd5 16 Ne4, Be6 17 Nc4, Ra6 led to a quick draw in Levitina-Semenova, Women's candidate match 1984).

12 ... c6

This natural move is almost always played. It frees the other knight to leave its defensive post at e7 and also enables the Black queen to reach the queenside. Occasionally you will also see **12..Nb6**, which also frees the knights and, in addition, relieves queenside pressure against b7. But it has the drawback of withdrawing a well-placed piece. Following **12...Nb6 13 Bd3** there could follow:

(a) **13...Bf5**, which is tactically based on **14 Rxe7, Bxd3**. Then **15 Rae1, Bf5!** leaves White in control of the e-file but without an immediate point of penetration, e.g. **16 Ng5, Bg6** as in Leonhardt-Suchting, Vienna 1908. White can try **17 Ndf3** with the idea of **18 Nh4**.

(Note that the immediate retreat to f5, 15...Bg6?, allows White an edge with 16 Nh4!, Nd5 17 Nxg6, hxg6 18 R7e5, Nb6 19 Nf3 or 16...Nc8 17 Nxg6, hxg6 18 R7e5 and the mating threat of Nf3-g5 and Qh3 won swiftly in Bastian-Eng, Bad Neuenahr 1984 — 18...Qxd4 19 Nf3, Qd7 20 Ng5, Nd6 21 Qb4! f6 22 Re7, Qb5 23 Rxg7 ch! and wins because 23...Kx-g7 24 Re7 ch, Kh8 25 Qh4 ch mates and 24...Nf7 hangs the queen).

(b) **13...Ned5**, completes a transfer of knights. But White can then maneuver knights to c5 and e5 and this should provide some superiority in minor pieces: **14 Ne4, Bf5 15 Nc5, Bxd3 16 Qxd3, Rb8 17 Ne5**, as in Nun-Sarwinski, Naleczow 1987.

(c) **13...Nf5** misplaces this knight and prevents the remaining Black bishop from emerging on a good square. After **14 Qc2, g6 15 Ne4** (Mestel-Hindle, British Championship 1972) White holds a slight edge.

(d) **13...Nc6**, aiming at d4 but keeping the c8-f5

diagonal open, is probably best. Then **14 Racl** and **15 Bbl** followed by Qc2 is dangerous but untested.

13 Ne4

The old books recommend **13 a4**, with queenside pressure, citing such games as Rossolimo-Reissman, San Juan 1967 — a modern evergreen game: **13...b6? 14 Ne5, Bb7 15 a5, Rc8 16 Ne4, Qc7 17 a6!, Ba8 18 Qh3, Nf4 19 Qg4, Ned5 20 Ra3, Ne6? 21 Bxd5, cxd5 22 Nf6 ch, Kh8 23 Qg6!!** (Page Frank Marshall: 23...fxg6 24 Nxg6 ch and mate next), **Qc2 24 Rh3!** Resigns.

The problem with this is that **13 a4** can be handled fairly easily by **13...Qb6** with a quick trade of queens and relative equality, e.g. **14 a5, Qxb3 15 Nxb3, Rd8 16 Nc5, Rb8 17 Ne5, Kf8 and 18...b6** (Rossolimo-Unzicker, Heidelberg 1949). To play **13 a4** White must be willing to try **18 Ra3** (e.g. **18...b6 19 axb6, axb6 20 Rf3!**) or avoid the queen trade with **13 a4, Qb6 14 Qa3!?** as in Low-Mandl, Bavarian Championship 1991 which went **14...Ng6 15 a5, Qd8 16 Ne4, Ngf4 17 a6, b6 18 Ne5** with advantage.

13 ... h6

The Siberian grandmaster Yevgeny Sveshnikov began a revival of **13 Ne4** in the late 1970's. Previously an old analysis by Grigory Levenfish held that **13 Ne4, Nb6** was dead even, e.g. **14 Nc5, Nxc4 15 Qxc4, b6 16 Nd3, Qd6**. However, there is no reason for White to surrender his bishop for the knight that is in partial retirement at b6. Sveshnikov showed that **13...Nb6 14 Bd3!** was promising.

What about **13...Qb6**, the move that equalizes in so many similar lines? Sveshnikov-Chekhov, Sochi 1983 went **14**

Qa3, Bg4! 15 Ne5, Qxd4! and Black had no troubles (16 Bxd5, Qxe5!; 16 Nxg4, Qxc4).

Afterwards, Sveshnikov suggested meeting **13...Qb6** with Bogolyubov's old idea of **14 Nc3!**, thereby breaking the blockade at d5: **14...Qxb3 15 Bxb3** and now **15...Be6 16 Ng5** or **15...Bg4 16 Nxd5, Nxd5 17 Bxd5!, exd5 18 Re7** with an excellent good knight-versus-bad-bishop endgame. See Illustrative Game (3).

Black has two other options but White seems to obtain an edge against either one fairly simply with Ne5 or Nc6. On **13...Qc7 14 Ne5, Bf5 15 a4** White has established solid control of open lines (15...Bxe4 16 Rxe4, Rad8 17 Rd1 favored White in Packroff-Scheglmann, Correspondence 1988).

And **13...Nb6 14 Nc5!, Nac4 15 Qxc4** allows the knights to cramp Black's position (15...b6 16 Nd3, Be6 17 Rxe6! or 16...Qd6 17 Qb4! as suggested by Porreca).

14 Ne5

Sveshnikov has also played **14 a4** with the idea of gaining space with **15 a5**. If Black responds **14...Qb6** then **15 Qa3!** avoids the endgame favorably. Better is **14...a5** and then **15 Ne5, Qb6 16 Qxb6, Nxb6**. In Sveshnikov-Dorfman, USSR Championship 1977 White went in for **17 Bxf7 ch, Rxf7 18 Nxf7, Kxf7 19 Nd6 ch, Kf8 20 Ra3** but only drew.

Better, Sveshnikov suggested, was **17 Nd6, Nxc4 18 Nexc4, Nd5 19 Re5** with an edge.

14 ... Qb6
15 Nd6

Also leading to a slight edge is **15 Rad1**. One point of **15 Nd6** is that **15...Qxd4** is met by **16 Qa3** with a dangerous threat of **Nexf7**.

15	**...**	**Qxb3**
16	**Bxb3**	

Thus far we are following van der Wiel-Karpov, Amsterdam 1980 which White lost although he stood better for several moves. Play continued **16...Rb8 17 Re2, Nf5 18 Nxf5, Bxf5 19 Bxd5!, cxd5 20 g4!** and now **20...Be6 21 f4!** leads to a significant edge for White, whereas Karpov's **20...Bh7 21 Rae1** leads to a minor one.

Illustrative Games:

(1) Leonhardt-Burn, Karlsbad 1911 —

1 e4, e5 2 Nf3, Nc6 3 Bc4, Bc5 4 c3, d6?! 5 d4, exd4 6 cxd4, Bb6 (The check has no point without...Nf6.) **7 Nc3, Nf6 8 0-0, 0-0 9 Bb3, Bg4 10 Be3, h6 11 Qd3, Re8 12 Nd2, Qe7 13 Rae1, Rad8 14 a3, Qf8 15 f4, Bc8** (Black has a typically cramped game and White has a free hand for king side expansion.) **16 h3, Kh8 17 g4!, Ne7 18 Kh1, d5 19 e5, Nh7 20 f5, f6 21 e6, c6 22 Bf4, Ng8 23 Na4, Ba5 24 Bc2, Qe7 25 Qg3, b5 26 Nc5, Bb6 27 b4, Nf8 28 a4!, a5 29 N2b3!, bxa4 30 Nxa5, Bxc5 31 Nxc6,** (Black is lost — 31...Qb7 32 Nxd8.) **Bxd4 32 Nxe7, Rxe7 33 Bc7, Be5 34 Rxe5!, Rxc7 35 Rxd5, Bb7 36 Qxc7, Bxd5 ch 37 Kg1, Re8 38 Bxa4, Re7 39 Qb8, Nh7 40 Rd1, Rb7 41 Qxb7!, Bxb7 42 Rd8 Resigns**

(2) Miles-Korchnoi, South Africa 1979 –

1 e4, e5 2 Nf3, Nc6 3 Bc4, Bc5 4 c3, Nf6 5 d4, exd4 6 cxd4, Bb4 ch 7 Bd2, Bxd2 ch 8 Nbxd2, d5 9 exd5, Nxd5 10 Qb3, Nce7 11 0-0, 0-0 12 Ne5, c6 13 Ne4, Qb6 14 Rad1, Qxb3 15 Bxb3, Rd8 16 Rfe1, Kf8 17 f3, f6 18 Nc4, b6 19 Kf2, Ba6 20 g4?, Rd7 21 g5?, Bxc4! 22 Bxc4, f5 23 Nc3, Nf4 (Black holds the edge even after 24 Kg3!, Nh5 ch 25 Kh4, g6.) **24 Ne2, Nxe2 25 Rxe2, Rad8 26 Ke3** (On 26 Red2 Black wins with 26...f4 followed by planting a knight on e3.), **b5! 27 Be6, Rd6 28 Kf4, Rxd4 ch 29 Rxd4, Rxd4 ch 30 Ke5, c5 31 Bb3, Rd8 32 Be6, Nc6 33 Kf4, Nd4 34 Re5, g6** (But not 34...Nxe6 ch 35 Rxe6 when White has counterplay.) **35 Bd5, a5 36 b3, Rd7 37 a4, c4! 38 bxc4, bxa2./*4 39 Re3, Re7! 40 Rxe7, Kxe7 41 Ke3, a3 42 c5, Nc2 ch White resigns.** White made too many mistakes, **20 g4?** and **21 g5?**

(3) Tamborini-Leoni, Correspondence 1990 –

1 e4, e5 2 Nf3, Nc6 3 Bc4, Bc5 4 c3, Nf6 5 d4, exd4 6 cxd4, Bb4 ch 7 Bd2, Bxd2 ch 8 Nbxd2, d5 9 exd5, Nxd5 10 Qb3, Nce7 11 0-0, 0-0 12 Rfe1, c6 13 Ne4, Qb6 14 Nc3, Qxb3 15 Bxb3, Bg4 16 Nxd5, Nxd5 17 Bxd5, cxd5 18 Re7, b5 19 Ne5, Be6 20 Rc1, Rfe8 21 Rec7, a6 22 f3, Rec8 23 Kf2, f6 24 Nd3, Rxc7 25 Rxc7, Rc8 26 Rxc8 ch, Bxc8 27 Nc5, Kf7 28 b4, g5 29 Ke3, h5 30 f4!, h4 31 g3, hxg3 32 hxg3, Ke8 33 Kf3, g4 ch? (A faulty bid to lock the king out.) **34 Ke3, Kd8 35 f5!, Bxf5 36 Nxa6, Bb1 37 a3, Be4 38 Kf4, Bg6 39 Kxg4, Resigns.**

CHAPTER TWO

INTRODUCTION
MOELLER ATTACK

1 e4, e5 2 Nf3, Nc6 3 Bc4, Bc5 4 c3, Nf6 5 d4, exd4 6 cxd4, Bb4 ch 7 Nc3

This introduces the Moeller Attack, one of the most intensely analyzed variations in history. It has been periodically declared refuted, most recently in the late 1960's after a Lajos Portisch improvement. But like a phoenix, the Moeller has always risen again.

7 ... Nxe4

The only move to test White's play. Routine responses such as **7...0-0** are bound to get Black killed after **8 e5 or 8 d5, e.g. 8 e5, Ne4 9 0-0!, Nxc3 10 bxc3** with an improved version of the positions cited in the note to Black's eighth move in the main line below (10...Bxc3 11 Ng5!, Bxa1 12 Qh5, h6

13 Nxf7).

Before the turn of the century **7...d5 8 exd5, Nxd5** was considered adequate. But then the strength of the thematic **9 0-0!** was appreciated. White threatens to win a piece and:

(a) **9...Nxc3 10 bxc3, Bxc3?** walks into a typical Giuoco crush — **11 Qb3!, Bxa1 12 Bxf7 ch, Kf8 13 Ba3 ch, Ne7 14 Bh5, g6** — else 15 Qf7 mate — **15 Ng5, Qe8 16 Re1** and wins (16...gxh5 17 Qf3 ch).

Black can avoid the worst of this by refusing the poisoned pawn, with **9...Be7**. However, **10 Bf4** gives White a superior center, better open lines to exploit and a lead in development.

(b) **9...Bxc3 10 bxc3, Nxc3?** loses a piece to **11 Qe1 ch**, but **10...0-0** also runs into trouble after **11 Qc2!**, threatening **12 Ng5**. On **11...h6 12 Re1, Be6?!** White has nice a combination in **13 Bxh6** (Steinitz-Schiffers, match 1896), **gxh6 14 Rxe6, fxe6 15 Qg6 ch** followed by **16 Qxh6 ch, 17 Qxe6 ch** and **18 Bxd5**.

(c) **9...Nb6** preserves minor pieces but, as usual, the knight is misplaced here. After **10 Re1 ch, Be7 11 Bb3, 0-0 12 d5!** Black's pieces continue the withdrawal.

(d) **9...Be6!** is best but it never really survived the famous brilliancy prize game Steinitz-von Bardeleben, Hastings 1895. White obtains a furious initiative by way of a series of exchanges: **10 Bg5, Be7 11 Bxd5, Bxd5 12 Nxd5, Qxd5 13 Bxe7, Nxe7 14 Re1, f6** (Intending to castle by hand, i.e. ...Kf7.) and now better than Steinitz's **15 Qe2, Qd7 16 Rac1 is 15 Qa4 ch, Kf7** (15...c6 16 Qb4! with a strong pin.) **16 Ne5 ch!**, as suggested by Yakov Estrin, or **15 Qe2, Qd7 16 Rad1!** so that **16...Kf7** allows **17 Qc4 ch, Nd5 18 Ne5 ch!**,

fxe5 19 dxe5 as pointed out by Igor Zaitsev.

8 0-0!

Greco had analyzed this back in the early 1600's after which his analysis was largely ignored for two and a half centuries. (Only 7 Bd2 is mentioned in, for example, Bird's 1877 survey of the openings.) A typical Greco example went **8 0-0, Nxc3?! 9 bxc3, Bxc3? 10 Qb3, Bxa1?? 11 Bxf7 ch, Kf8 12 Bg5, Ne7 13 Ne5!, Bxd4** (Or 13...d5 14 Qf3, Bf5 15 Be6, g6 16 Bh6 ch, Ke8 17 Bf7, mate.) **14 Bg6!, d5 15 Qf3 ch, Bf5 16 Bxf5, Bxe5 17 Be6 ch, Bf6 18 Bxf6, gxf6 19 Qxf6 ch, Ke8 20 Qf7 mate.**

See next note for more on **8...Nxc3.**

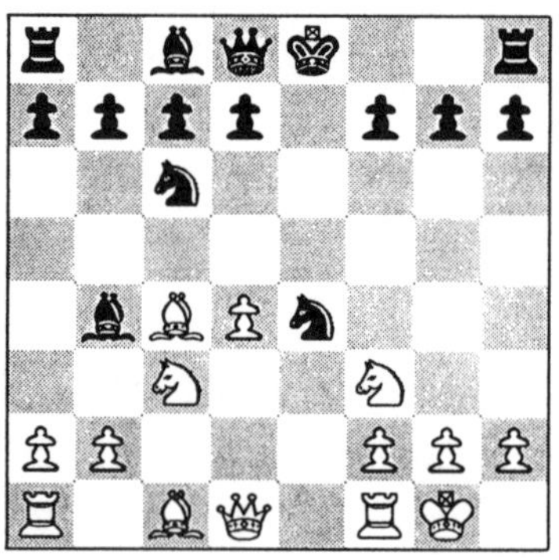

8 ... Bxc3

Only two other moves have been tried here. One is the clever **8...0-0**, based on regaining the piece via **9 Nxe4, d5.** However, **8...0-0 9 d5!** is a simple refutation since to avoid dropping material Black must play something like **9...Bxc3 10 bxc3, Ne7 11 Re1, Nf6 12 d6!** as in Spielmann-Cohn, Carlsbad 1907. The blocking d5-d6 idea is a common one in such positions. Even if Black plays **11...Nf6** he gets the same kind of middlegame — a pawn up but without queenside development. (Even worse is 8...0-0 9 d5, Nxc3 10 bxc3, Bxc3 11 Bg5, Ne7 12 d6!.)

The other major alternative is **8...Nxc3?! 9 bxc3** and now on **9...Bxc3 10 Qb3** Black can improve on Greco's analysis from the previous note with **10...d5! 11 Bxd5, 0-0** with survival chances. This defensive finesse — avoiding the gain of material in order to throw in ...d7-d5 — is another common one in the Giuoco, just as d5-d6 is for the attack.

However, White, too, can improve. After **8...Nxc3 9 bxc3, Bxc3** he plays **10 Ba3!**, to trap the enemy king in the center. For example, **10...d5 11 Bb5, Bxa1 12 Re1 ch, Be6 13 Qa4** with a terrific attack, e.g. **13...Rb8? 14 Ne5!** or **13...Qb8! 14 Ne5, a6 15 Qg4!** followed by **Qxg7** or **Nxf7**.

The key variation, analyzed in the 1930s by the Scottish master J.M. Aitken, runs **10 Ba3, d6 11 Rc1, Ba5 12 Qa4!, a6** (Threatening ...b7-b5, else 13 d5 wins.) **13 Bd5, Bb6 14 Rxc6!, Bd7** (14...bxc6 15 Qxc6 ch.) **15 Re1 ch, Kf8 16 Rxd6!, cxd6 17 Bxd6 ch, Kg8 18 Ng5!, g6** (18...Qxg5 19 Qxd7 and mate on e8 or f7.) **19 Bxf7 ch, Kg7 20 Be5 ch, Kh6 21 Ne6!, Bxa4 22 Bg7 ch** and White mates in six more moves.

One conclusion we can draw from this is that if Black is going to play **8...Nxc3 9 bxc3** then he must fight differently at the ninth move and the only serious alternative is **9...d5!**

Black strives to complete his development while rejecting material gain. The drawback is that White can offer a piece sacrifice with **10 cxb4, dxc4 11 Re1 ch, Ne7** (11...Be6?? 12 d5) **12 Bg5, f6 13 Qe2!**. If the offer is accepted — **13...fxg5 14 Qxc4** White's attack appears very strong but there is little experience to prove this (14...Rf8 15 Re5!, g4 16 Ng5, h6 17 Nh7, Rf7 18 Rae1, Qd6 19 Rex7 ch, Rxe7 20 Qg8 ch, Kd7 21 Nf8 ch, Kc6 22 Qc4 ch etc. — analysis by Rosenzweig).

The rejection of the sacrifice by **13...0-0** has been tried in games like Schwarz-Teschner, Berlin 1949 which led to a draw after **14 Qxe7, fxg5 15 Qc5, Qf6 16 Nxg5, Qxf2 ch 17 Kh1, Bg4 18 Qxc4 ch, Kh8 19 Rf1, Be2! 20 Nf7 ch** etc. White can improve on this with 16 d5 (16...g4 17 Ne5 or 16...Bf5 17 Nd4).

There is also analysis, again not backed up by master play, suggesting Black's best is **13...Bg4 14 Bf4, Kf7!** (An improvement over 14...Qd7 15 Qxc4, Bxf3 16 gxf3, c6 17 Rac1, Kf8 18 b5, cxb5 19 Qb4!, a5 20 Qd6, Rd8 21 Rc7 and wins—Estrin-Klaman, Leningrad 1951.)

After **14...Kf7!** there follows **15 Qxc4 ch, Nd5 16 Nd2!** (Better than 16 Bxc7, Rc8!) which leads to a position regarded by Paul Keres and other analysts as favorable for White: **16...Be6 17 Bg3, Re8 18 Ne4** followed by **Nc5** (Or 18...b6 19 Rac1, Qd7 20 Bxc7 and Nd6 ch.).

That leaves us with one key line — **8...Bxc3!**, the one regarded as most dangerous to White since the days of Greco.

9 d5!

This is the move analyzed by Jorgen Moeller in 1898, that overturned opinions on the Giuoco. When Steinitz had revived **7 Nc3** at Hastings 1895 his idea was to play **9 bxc3** and on **9...d5!**, respond with **10 Ba3**. He believed Black had nothing better than **10...Be6 11 Bb5, Nd6** as in a Steinitz-Schlechter game.

However, Steinitz learned the hard way that his analysis was faulty. In their third game of his return match with Emanuel Lasker, 1896, Black accepted the temporary piece sacrifice and ended up a clear pawn ahead: **10 Ba3, dxc4 11 Re1, Be6! 12 Rxe4, Qd5! 13 Qe2, 0-0-0** etc.

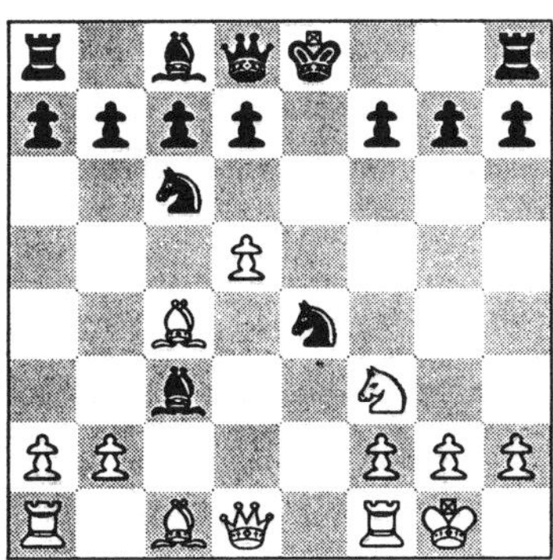

9 ... Ne5

We'll consider the main line of the Moeller Attack (9...Bf6!) in the next chapter. But there are at least four other moves worthy of being considered. Of the four, only the last threatens to equalize. Let's count them:

(a) **9...Na5** has the drawback of putting this knight offsides (Compared with 9...Ne5 in footnote "e", into which White can now transpose with 10 cxb4?!). Best is **10 Bd3!** after which **10...Nc5 11 bxc3, Nxd3** (11...0-0 allows the ancient

12 Bxh7 ch! combination.) **12 Qxd3, 0-0 13 Ng5!** threatening mate on h7 and ensuring a strong attack, e.g. **13...g6 14 Qh3, h5 15 Ne4 or 13...f5 14 d6!**.

(b) **9...Ne7** keeps the knight in a position for defense. But the real problem is the other knight after **10 bxc3.** Inevitably it will have to retreat, and if it retreats to d6 then it will block the development of the queenside pieces, while if it retreats to f6, White's d-pawn is free to be sacrificed. For example, **10 bxc3, 0-0 11 Re1, Nf6 12 d6!** with a fine game for White (12...cxd6 13 Bg5, Nf5? 14 Bd3).

Black may do a little better with **10...Nd6** but after **11 Bb3, 0-0 12 c4**, he has problems with his remaining undeveloped pieces (12...b6 13 Bb2, Ne8 14 Bc2, Ng6 15 Qd3, d6 16 Nd4 with advantage to White, as Moeller pointed out).

(c) **9...Nd6** gives White a choice of pieces to capture, while attacking the c4-bishop. After **10 dxc6, Nxc4 11 Qe2 ch**, however, White regains a piece favorably (11...Qe7 12 Qxc4, Ba5 13 Bg5! and Rae1).

Black must meet **10 dxc6** with a bishop retreat, such as **10...Bf6**, which allows Black to meet **11 Re1 ch** with **11...B-e7**. Then, however, **12 Bg5, f6 13 Ne5!** leads to a winning attack according to analysis by Wolfgang Unzicker: **13...fxe5 14 Rxe5, Nf5 15 Qh5 ch, g6 16 Rxf5!!** or **13...Kf8 14 cxd7, Bxd7 15 Nxd7 ch, Qxd7 16 Bh4.**

(d) **9...Ba5** has the advantage over the various knight moves and also over **9...Bf6** of controlling the e1 square that so often White uses for pins or rook-checks. White does best now to play **10 dxc6** with a threat of forking pieces with **11 Qd5** or **11 Qa4**, e.g. **10...0-0 11 Qd5, Nd6 12 Bd3, Bb6 13 Bxh7 ch!, Kxh7 14 Qh5 ch, Kg8 15 Ng5** with the usual deadly attack.

Similarly, **10...dxc6 11 Qa4, Bb6** and now **12 Bxf7 ch, Kxf7 13 Qxe4 and 14 Ng5 ch** must favor White.

The critical alternative is **10...bxc6!** (Allowing Black to play 13...d5! in the line cited above.). White does better with **11 Ne5** since **11...0-0** loses to **12 Nxf7, Rxf7 13 Bxf7 ch, Kxf7 14 Qh5 ch** picking up the a5 bishop. Therefore, **11 Ne5** is best met by the defensive **11...Nd6** and then **12 Qg4, Qf6** (12...0-0? 13 Bg5!, Qe8 14 Bf6 and wins) **13 b4** followed by posting a bishop on b2, e.g. **13...Bxb4 14 Bb2, Nxc4 15 Qxc4**.

This is better than **13...Qxe5** as given in an ancient analysis in the German "Handbuch" **14 Bf4, Qf6 15 Rae1 ch, Kf8 16 Bg5, Qg6 17 Be7 ch, Kg8 18 Bxd6!, Bb7** (19 Re8 mate was threatened) **19 Qxd7, h5 20 Bc5** etc.

Analysis in New In Chess gives Black the edge after **13...Nxc4 14 Nxc4, Bxb4 15 Bg5, Qe6** but **15 Bb2** may improve.

That's a lot of analysis but not that much of it really has to be memorized to play the Moeller Attack. Let's return to **9...Ne5**.

10	**bxc3**	**Nxc4**
11	**Qd4**	

(See diagram, next page)

11	**...**	**0-0**

White must regain his sacrificed piece and should obtain at least a slight edge against any move here. The attempt to keep material with **11...Ncd6?** gets Black a bad game after **12 Qxg7,**

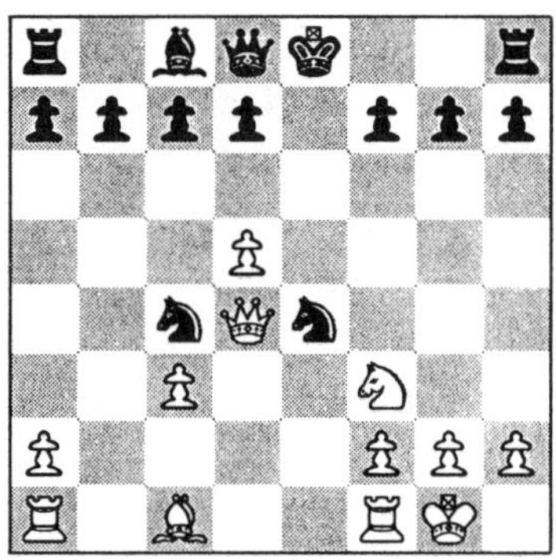

(Position after 11 Qd4)

Qf6 (or 12...Rf8 13 Bh6, Qe7 14 Qxh7) **13 Qxf6, Nxf6 14 Re1 ch, Kf8? 15 Bh6 ch, Kg8 16 Re5!**, threatening Rg5 mate, or **14...Nfe4 15 Nd2, f5 16 f3.**

A lot of attention has been paid to the alternative of **11...f5 12 Qxc4** (Not 12 Bg5, Nxg5 13 Qxg7 because of 13...Rf8! 14 Nxg5, Qf6!), **d6 13 Nd4, 0-0 14 f3** after which White's chances have been shown to be preferable in experience spread over seven decades:

(a) **14...Nf6 15 Bg5, Bd7 16 Rae1** and Black has difficulty developing his heavy pieces.

(b) **14...Nc5 15 Re1, Re8 16 Ba3, Rxe1 ch 17 Rxe1, Na6 18 Qb5!** and Black is becoming paralyzed.

(c) **14...Nc5 15 Re1, Kh8! 16 Ba3, b6** and now **17 Nc6, Ba6! 18 Qd4, Qg5 19 Bxc5** favored White in Romanov-Kotov, correspondence 1964 but **17 Bxc5!** is clearer: **17...bxc5 18 Nc6, Qg5 19 Re7, Bb7 20 Rae1, Qd2 21**

R7e2!, Qg5 22 Na5, Bc8 23 f4! and 24 Qb5 dominates the board. Similarly, **17...dxc5 18 Nc6, Qg5 19 Re7, Bb7 20 Rael, Qd2 21 Qh4!, Qxd5 22 Ne5.**

12 Qxe4 b5

This was Karpov's attempt at an improvement over the old idea of **12...Nd6**, e.g. Mieses-Suchting, Vienna 1908, which went **13 Qd3, Ne8 14 c4, d6 15 Bb2, f5 16 Rael, Nf6 17 Nd4**, and Black untangled himself with great difficulty, or **13 Qf4, Ne8 14 d6!** as in Kopylov-Levenfish, USSR Championship 1949 (14...cxd6 15 Ba3, b6 16 Rfel and Nd4).

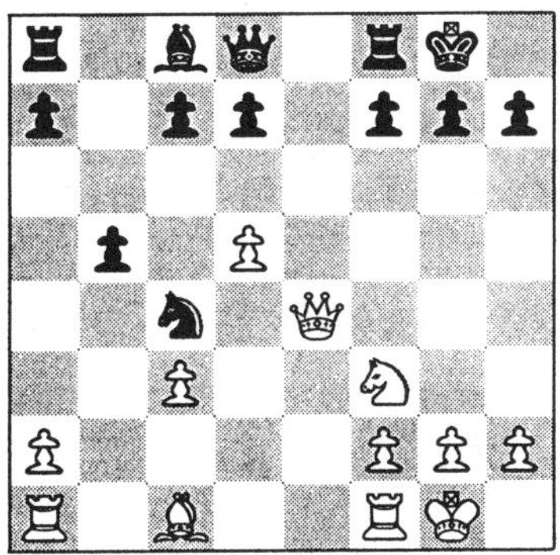

13 a4!

However, White retains an initiative thanks to this stroke against the queenside. In a game from the 1988 World Action Championship, Dzindzhichashvili-Karpov, Black remained on the defensive after **13...c6 14 axb5, cxd5 15 Qd4!, Nb6 16 Be3, d6 17 Ra2!** followed by doubling rooks on the a- or e-file. For the rest of the game, see the introduction.

This concludes our survey of the alternatives to the main thicket of Moeller analysis. If your opponent is unwary of Giuoco analysis he may be caught in one of the alternative notes above and never make it out of the opening.

If, however, he is booked-up, he will be capable of blitzing off the first 15 moves of the Moeller attack and then the real game begins.

Illustrative Games:

(4) Lasker-N.N., simultaneous exhibition, London 1908 -
1 e4, e5 2 Nf3, Nc6 3 Bc4, Bc5 4 c3, Nf6 5 d4, exd4 6 cxd4, Bb4 ch 7 Nc3, Nxe4 8 0-0, Bxc3 9 d5, Na5? 10 bxc3?!, 0-0 11 Bd3 (Transposing into note "a" to Black's ninth move above.), **Rc8 12 Rc1, Nc5 13 Bc2, d6 14 Bg5, Rxe1 ch 15 Qxe1, f6 16 Be3, Nd7 17 Qe2, Ne5 18 Nxe5, dxe5 19 Rd1** (An important preparatory move for the coming sacrifice.), **b6 20 Qh5, g6 21 Bxg6, hxg6 22 Qxg6 ch, Kf8?** (22...Kh8 had to be tried) **23 Bh6 ch, Ke7 24 Bg7, Qd6 25 Qh7, Be6 26 Bxf6 ch!?, Kxf6 27 Rd3, Bxd5 28 Rh3, Qf8 29 Rh6 ch, Kg8 30 Qg6 ch, Kf4 31 Rh4 mate.**

(5) Estrin-Slatin, Tula 1938 —
1 e4, e5 2 Nf3, Nc6 3 Bc4, Bc5 4 c3, Nf6 5 d4, exd4 6 cxd4, Bb4 ch 7 Nc3, Nxe4 8 0-0, Bxc3 9 d5, Na5? 10 Bd3!, Nc5 11 bxc3, Nxd3 12 Qxd3, 0-0 13 Ng5!, f5 14 d6!

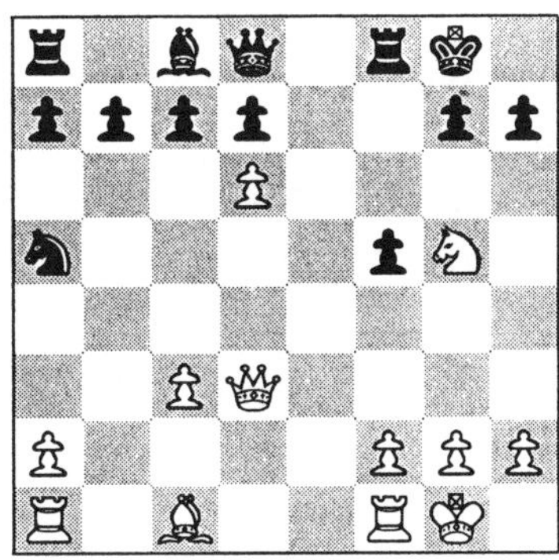

14...c6 15 Re1, h6 16 Re7!, hxg5 17 Bxg5, Rf7 18 Rae1! (Better than 18 Rxf7, Qxg5 19 Rxf5, Qd8 20 Re1 which should still win.)**, Rxe7 19 Rxe7, Qf8 20 Bh6!, gxh6** (Or 20...Qf6 21 Bxg7!, Qxg7 22 Qxf5! and wins.) **21 Qg3 ch, Kh8 22 Qg6, Resigns.**

CHAPTER THREE

THE OLD MAIN MOELLER

(after 1 e4, e5 2 Nf3, Nc6 3 Bc4, Bc5 4 c3, Nf6 5 d4, exd4 6 cxd4, Bb4 ch 7 Nc3, Nxe4 8 0-0, Bxc3 9 d5!)

9 ... Bf6

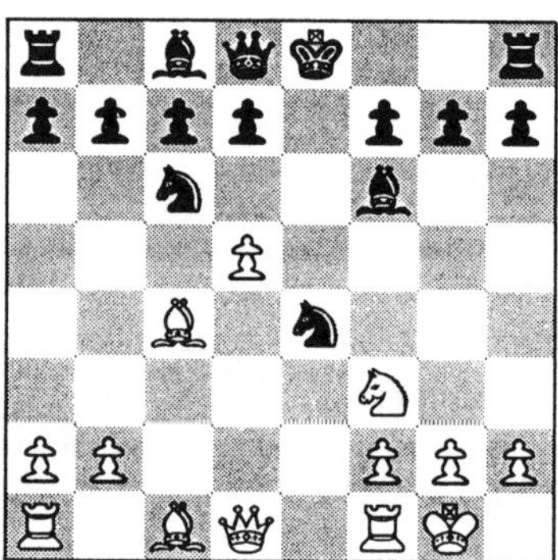

This is by far the most difficult line. He allows White to post a rook on e1 because he will be able to castle quickly (e.g. 10 dxc6?, bxc6! 11 Re1, d5! and Black's anchored knight and extra pawn give him a clear advantage).

10 Re1 Ne7

If Black intends to reach the old main Moeller line (10...0-0 11 Rxe4, Ne7) this is simply a different move order (10...Ne7 11 Rxe4, 0-0). The chief value of **10...Ne7** is to permit Black to enter the complexities of **10...Ne7 11 Rxe4, d6 12 Bg5, Bxg5 13 Nxg5, h6!**.

It should be pointed out that Black's knight has no better place to be than on e7, regardless of which subvariation we investigate. For example, **10...0-0 11 Rxe4, Na5?** simply exiles the knight offstage for a large part of the middlegame — **12 Bd3, d6 13 g4!** — a bayonet thrust that works well in such positions.

After **13...c5 14 g5, Be7 15 Bd2** Black can't play **15...Bf5** because of **16 Bxa5** and **17 Ra4**. So **15...b6 16 Qe2, Bf5 17 Re1!** was played in A.R.B. Thomas-Markwell, correspondence 1964-65, which resulted in a victory for White soon after **17...c4** (17...Re8 18 Bb5 or 17...Bxe4 18 Qxe4 is worse) **18 Bc2, Re8 19 Ba4, Bd7 20 Bxd7, Qxd7 21 Nh4!, Kf8 22 Qf3, Kg8 23 Qe3, Kf8 24 Bc3 and Qd4.**

11 Rxe4 d6

Now on **11...0-0** White cannot enter the main line with **12 Bg5** because then **12...Nf5!** is strong. However, chess can be a fair game: If your opponent stops one of your ideas, it is likely he is allowing another. In this case, **11...0-0** allows a strong **12 d6!**, exploiting lack of enemy queenside development.

Then after **12...Ng6** White harasses the knight with **13 h4!**, see Illustrative Game (7) below. Therefore **12...cxd6** is usually played, in the hopes of securing a draw by way of **13 Qxd6, Nf5 14 Qd5, Ne7!**.

However, White need not cooperate so fully. He should avoid **11...0-0 12 d6, cxd6** and now **13 Bf4** because again Black can do well by giving back his d-pawns — **13...d5 14 Bxd5, Nxd5 15 Qxd5, d6!** and **16...Be6**.

But he can meet **12...cxd6** with **13 Bg5!** after which **13...Nf5** allows a dangerous **14 Qd5!, g6 15 Rae1!** (15...Bxg5 16 Re8!) and the surrender of material with **13...d5 14 Bxd5, Nxd5 15 Qxd5, d6** now allows **16 Bxf6, Qxf6 17 Rd4 or 17 Nd4** with good compensation (Estrin).

Also possible is **13 Bg5, Bxg5 14 Nxg5**, when **14...h6?** — a move that works for Black in similar Moeller positions — is actually a blunder here because of **15 Nxf7!, Rxf7 16 Bxf7 ch, Kxf7 17 Qh5 ch** and Black resigned in Pyrlja-Bohm, correspondence 1975 because of **17...Kg8 18 Rae1** or **17...Ng6 18 Rf4 ch** with a win in either case. Better is **14...d5 15 Bxd5, Nxd5 16 Qxd5, d6** although **17 Rae1** is still problemsome.

12 Bg5

Another thematic idea in such positions is **12 g4** (see Lazard-Gibaud from the introduction). But the more forceful **12 Bg5** has been analyzed more.

12 ... Bxg5

Black cannot easily avoid this since the doubling of his f-pawns is a severe weakness [12...0-0 13 Bxf6, gxf6 — see Illustrative Game (6)].

If Black prepares instead to castle queenside with **12...Bf5** White can cross him up with **13 Bb5 ch!** (13...Kf8 14 Rf4 with advantage).

13 Nxg5

Now we have a parting of the ways: the older **13...0-0** is considered below, while the modern **13...h6!?** appears in the next chapter.

13 ... 0-0

The position has become trappy and many an unwary Black will play **13...Bf5?** and be surprised by **14 Qf3!**.

Then both **15 Qxf5** and **15 Rxe7 ch** are threatened, and the capture of the rook gets Black killed quickly via **14...Bx-e4 15 Qxf7 ch, Kd7 16 Qe6 ch, Ke8 17 Qxe4** followed by **18 Re1** or **Ne6**.

A better try is **14...Qd7** but then **15 Bb5!** leads to **15...Qxb5 16 Qxf5** with winning threats of **17 Qxf7 ch** and **17 Rae1**.

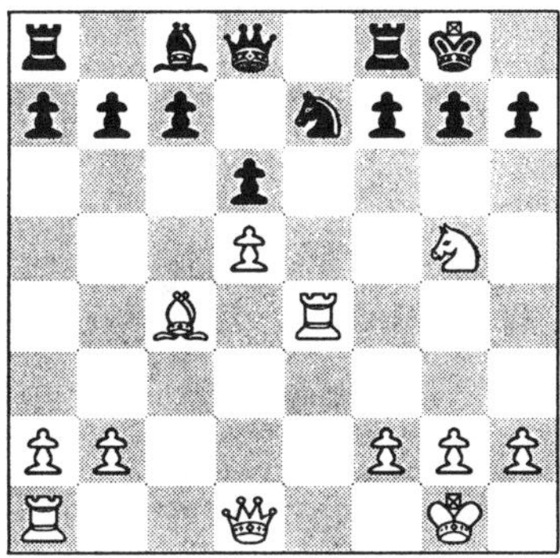

14 Nxh7!

Without this move the attack draws to a quick close.

14 ... Kxh7

Accepting the challenge. After **14...Bf5** White can

obtain equal material with **15 Rxe7, Qxe7 16 Nxf8** but the position is, if anything, easier for Black to play after **16...Rxf8 17 Rc1, c5! 18 Rc3, Re8 19 Re3, Qd7** (Tyroler-Bottlik, Budapest 1963).

The key line after **14...Bf5** is **15 Rh4!, Re8** (not 15...Bxh7? because 16 Qh5) **16 Qh5!, Ng6** (forced) **17 Rd4**. Now **17...Qd7 18 Ng5, Ne5 19 Rh4** is bad, so the best play for both sides is **17...Re5 18 f4, Nxf4! 19 Rxf4, Bg6 20 Qf3, Kxh7 21 Bd3** which is described as unclear by Harding and Botterill — a judgment that apparently has yet to be tested. However, it is not easy for Black to defend against the threat of doubling on the h-file, e.g. **21...Bxd3 22 Qh3 ch!, Kg8 23 Rh4 or 21...Qe7 22 Qh3 ch** (not 22 Rxf7??, Re1 ch 23 Kf2, Qh4 ch). Black's best appears to be **21...Kg8 22 Bxg6, fxg6** but **23 Raf1** retains an edge. See also Illustrative Game (10).

Note that **18...Re4** allows the attack to roll on with **19 Rxe4, Bxe4 20 Ng5, Qf6 21 Qh7 ch, Kf8 22 Nxe4, Qd4 ch 23 Nf2, Qxc4 24 f5, Ne7 25 f6!** (Andersson-Johansson, Sweden 1969).

15	**Qh5 ch**	**Kg8**
16	**Rh4**	**f5**

Black can also create a flight square with **16...f6**, endorsed by Bogolyubov. However, one of the guiding principles of these Moeller positions is that Black needs to fight for king side space. After **16...f6** White can respond **17 g4** with the side of **18 Bd3** and, if **18...f5**, then **19 g5** and perhaps **20 g6!**. An analysis by Keres runs **17 g4, Re8 18 Bd3, Kf8 19 Qh8 ch, Ng8** (19...Kf7 20 Qh5 ch) **20 Bh7, Kf7 21 Bg6 ch!, Kf8** and White can draw with **22 Bh7** if he wants to.

If he's more ambitious, he can try **17 Re1** (instead of 17 g4) with the idea of **18 Rhe4, Nf5 19 Re8**. On **17...Nf5 18 Bd3** (18...Nxh4?? 19 Bh7 ch, Kh8 20 Bg6 ch and mates) the game goes on.

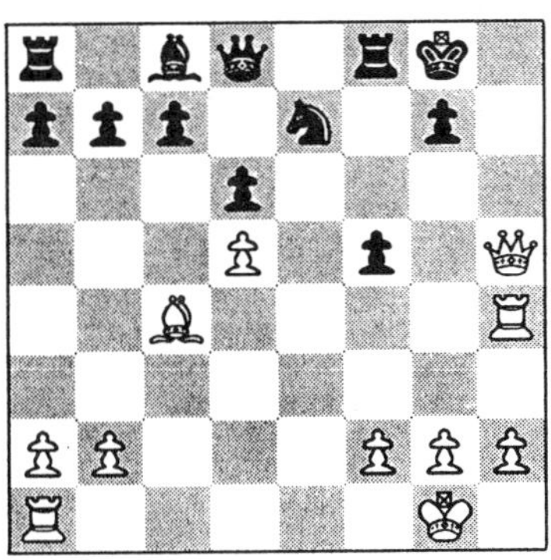

17 Qh7 ch

In recent years it's been widely suggested that **17 Rh3** is White's best chance, although Black can then virtually force a draw with **17...f4**. Then **18 Bd3** is met by **18...Bf5!** and **18 g4!? by 18...Bxg4! 19 Qxg4, Qc8**, so White must seek a perpetual check with **18 Qh7 ch, Kf7 19 Qh5 ch, Kg8**.

The only real advantage nowadays to White's playing that line (17 Rh3, f4 18 Qh7 ch, Kf7 19 Qh5 ch) is that he may catch Black napping. During the 1980's it was often suggested that 19...Ng6 is better than taking the perpetual check. It was claimed to either win for Black (in the *Informant* and elsewhere) or to favor Black solidly (*New In Chess* No. 5).

However, subsequent analysis (by Pantaleoni, *N.I.C.* No.

8) showed this was questionable because of **20 Bd3!**, e.g. **20...Qf6 21 Rf3!, Ke7** (21...Bg4? 22 Bxg6 ch, Qxg6 23 Rxf4 ch) **22 Bxg6, Bd7** (22...Qxb2? 23 Re1 ch, Kd8 24 Rxf4! and wins) **23 Re1 ch, Kd8 24 g3** and wins.

Or **20...Bxh3 21 Bxg6 ch, Kf6** (21...Ke7? 22 Qh4 ch) **22 gxh3, Qd7 23 Bh7, Qf7!** (Not 23...Rae8 24 Qg6 ch, Ke7 25 Qg5 ch, Rf6 26 Qxg7 ch, Rf7 27 Qg5 ch, Rf6 28 Bg6, Rf8 29 Re1 ch and White has winning chances.) **24 Qh4 ch, g5 25 Qh6 ch, Ke7 26 Qxg5 ch, Kd7 27 Bg6, Qf6** with an unclear position.

17 ... Kf7
18 Rh6!

This move, which prepares Be2-h5 ch and prevents a Black knight from going to g6, must be played here, rather than after **18 Re1, Ng6 19 Rh6** (When Black defends easily with 19...Qg5!). White's task is to keep Black from coordinating his pieces and completing queenside development — and only **18 Rh6** does that. There is also a cute tactical idea coming up involving Re6!.

18 ... Rg8

Black must find a way to anticipate the bishop check at h5. With **18...Rg8** he clears f8 for his king. Compare with **18...Bd7? 19 Be2!, Rg8 20 Bh5 ch, Kf8 21 Rf6 ch!** and mates.

19 Re1

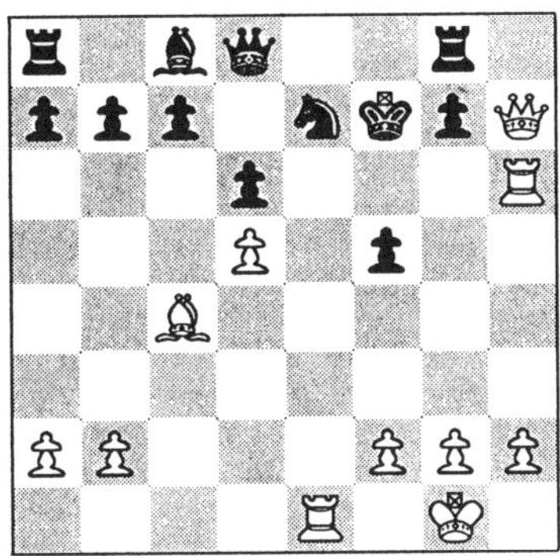

19 ... Kf8

This has been suggested as the best move — in fact, the best chance for Black to win. Actually, Black should start thinking about drawing.

He cannot defend with **19...Bd7** since then **20 Ree6!** is strong because of its threat of a check on f6. After **20...Bxe6 21 dxe6 ch, Kf8 22 Rf6 ch!, Ke8 23 Qh5 ch, g6 24 Qh7** does the trick. No better is **21...Ke8** immediately, since **22 Rg6!** and **Rxg7** wins.

Black's best may be **19...Qf8** so that **20 Be2** is met by **20...Ke8 21 Bh5 ch, Kd8**. Better is **20 Bb5**, cutting off the king's escape and threatening Ree6 (e.g. 20...a6? 21 Ree6!, axb5 22 Rhf6 ch, Ke8 23 Rxf8 ch, Rxf8 24 Re1!, Rxa2 25 Qxg7, and wins).

Black must meet **20 Bb5** with **20...Rh8! 21 Qxh8, gxh6 22 Qh7 ch, Kf6** and White can take a draw with **23 Rxe7, Qxe7 24 Qxh6 ch** and a perpetual check.

If White is going to find more in the position it might come from **20 Rh3** with the idea of **20 Rhe3**. Then **20...f4 21 Rh4, Bf5? 22 Rxf4** is strong but **21...Ke8** is hard to crack, e.g. **22 Bb5 ch, Kd8 23 Rxf4!, Qxf4 24 Qxg8 ch!** but Black has **22...Bd7**, which defends safely.

20 Rh3 Bd7

It's been known for some time that **20...f4?** is risky because of **21 Rh4** and, as Estrin pointed out in 1985, after **21...g5 22 Rh6, Nf5** — which supposedly forces a draw — White wins with the pretty **23 Re8 ch!!, Kxe8** (23...Qxe8 24 Rf6 ch, mates) **24 Qxg8 ch, Ke7 25 Rh7 ch, Kf6 26 Qxd8 ch.**

21 Rhe3 Nc8

Allowing the double capture on e7 is simply too risky — especially since Black lacks a useful alternative to **21...Nc8.** Ludek Pachman tried **21...b5 22 Bb3, a5?** in a 1992 game (versus Dueball) but ended up in a losing endgame after **23 Rxe7, Qxe7 24 Rxe7, Kxe7 25 Bc2, Raf8 26 f4!** followed by the queen's emergence on the queenside after **Qh4-e1**!

22 Bd3

Now **22...Nb6?** allows **23 Bxf5, Nxd5 24 Bxd7!, Nxe3 25 Be6** or **24...Qxd7 25 Rf3 ch.** Also bad is **22...Qf6?**, which allows **23 Bxf5!, Bxf5 24 Re8 ch.**

22 ... g6
23 h4

White cannot improve his position otherwise. Now **23...Nb6?** loses to **24 Re7** and **23...Be8?** to **24 Rxe8 ch.**

But Black can offer a draw with **23...Rg7 24 Qh8 ch, Rg8 25 Qh7, Rg7.**

Should White accept it? Theory indicates that if he plays **25 Qh6 ch** instead of **25 Qh7**, Black will continue **25...Kf7!** and now Vukovic's **26 Re6** is met by Keres' recommendation of **26...Qf8!**.

23	**...**	**Rg7**
24	**Qh8 ch**	**Rg8**
25	**Qh6 ch**	**Kf7**

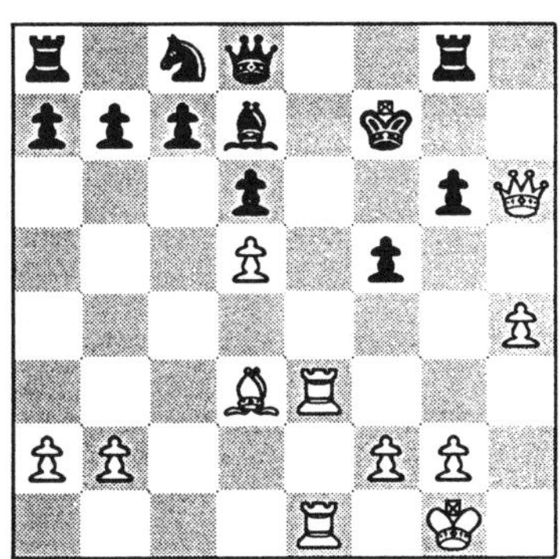

But **26 h5** is a winning try, e.g.:

(a) **26...gxh5 27 Qxh5 ch, Kf8** (27...Rg6 28 Rg3) **28 Bxf5;**

(b) **26...Qf8 27 Qh7 ch, Qg7 28 hxg6 ch, Kf8 29 Qh4;**

(c) **26...Qf6 27 Re6!, Bxe6 28 Rxe6.** Now most queen moves allow **29 hxg6 ch,** while giving up the queen with

28...Qxe6 29 dxe6 ch, Kxe6 is met by **30 Bc4 ch, d5 31 Qe3 ch, Kd6 32 Bxd5!**. Similar to that is **28...Ne7 29 Rxf6 ch, Kxf6** after which **30 Qe3, 30 hxg6** or **30 f4** all look promising for White.

Black should play **28...Qg7** when **Qg5** looks dangerous (29...Re8 30 hxg6 ch; 29...Qd4 30 h6; 29...Rf8 30 Rxg6) — but remains untested. White is, after all, a rook down.

Illustrative Games:

(6) Spielmann-Duras, Karlsbad 1907 —

1 e4, e5 2 Nf3, Nc6 3 Bc4, Bc5 4 c3, Nf6 5 d4, exd4 6 cxd4, Bb4 ch 7 Nc3, Nxe4 8 0-0, Bxc3 9 d5, Bf6 10 Re1, Ne7 11 Rxe4, d6 12 Bg5, 0-0? 13 Bxf6, gxf6 14 Nh4, Ng6 15 Qh5 (Now h7 is a permanent target.), **Kh8 16 Rae1, Bd7 17 Bd3, Rg8** (Intending...Rg7 to protect h7.) **18 Re7!, Rg7 19 Bxg6, fxg6 20 Nxg6 ch!, Kg8** (Of course, 20...Rxg6 21 Qxh7, mate.) **21 Rxg7 ch Resigns**, because of **22 Re7 ch.**

(7) Siecker-Popescu, Correspondence 1982 —

1 e4, e5 2 Nf3, Nc6 3 Bc4, Bc5 4 c3, Nf6 5 d4, exd4 6 cxd4, Bb4 ch 7 Nc3, Nxe4 8 0-0, Bxc3 9 d5, Bf6 10 Re1, Ne7 11 Rxe4, 0-0 12 d6, Ng6 13 h4!, Nxh4 14 Nxh4, Bxh4 15 Qh5!, Bf6 16 dxc7, Qxc7 17 Qxf7 ch! Resigns

(8) Ohls-Wagner, Correspondence 1929 —

1 e4, e5 2 Nf3, Nc6 3 Bc4, Bc5 4 c3, Nf6 5 d4, exd4 6 cxd4, Bb4 ch 7 Nc3, Nxe4 8 0-0, Bxc3 9 d5, Bf6 10 Re1, Ne7 11 Rxe4, d6 12 Bg5, Bxg5 13 Nxg5, 0-0 14 Nxh7, Kxh7 15 Rh4 ch, Kg8 16 Qh5, f5 17 Re1!?, Re8? (17...Ng6! is best so that 18 Rh3 Rf6 and Black defends against 19 Qh7 ch Kf7 20 Re6 with 20...Nf8.) **18**

Re6!, Kf8 19 g3!, c6 20 Rf6 ch!, gxf6 21 Qh6 ch, Kf7 22 Qh7 ch, Kf8 23 Rh6, Ng8 (23...Nxd5 24 Bxd5, cxd5 25 Rg6, Re1 ch 26 Kg2, Be6 27 Rg7! wins.) **24 Rg6, Re1 ch 25 Kg2** and wins.

(9) Karaklaic-Gligoric, Belgrade 1954 —

1 e4, e5 2 Nf3, Nc6 3 Bc4, Bc5 4 c3, Nf6 5 d4, exd4 6 cxd4, Bb4 ch 7 Nc3, Nxe4 8 0-0, Bxc3 9 d5, Bf6 10 Re1, Ne7 11 Rxe4, d6 12 Bg5, Bxg5 13 Nxg5, 0-0 14 Nxh7!, Kxh7 15 Qh5 ch, Kg8 16 Rh4, f5 17 Be2, Ng6? (Better is 17...Re8 and if 18 Re1 then 18...Kf8 19 Bb5, Bd7 20 Re6, Ng8!) **18 Qh7 ch, Kf7 19 Rh6, Nf4 Draw** (because of 20 Bh5 ch, Nxh5 21 Qg6 ch with a perpetual check).

(10) Walker-Robertson, British Correspondence Open 1988 —

1 e4, e5 2 Nf3, Nc6 3 Bc4, Bc5 4 c3, Nf6 5 d4, exd4 6 cxd4, Bb4 ch 7 Nc3, Nxe4 8 0-0, Bxc3 9 d5, Bf6 10 Re1, Ne7 11 Rxe4, d6 12 Bg5, Bxg5 13 Nxg5, 0-0 14 Nxh7, Bf5 15 Rh4, Re8 16 Qh5, Ng6 17 Rd4, Re5 18 f4, Nxf4! 19 Rxf4, Bg6 20 Qh3, (Attempting to improve over 20 Qf3.) **Qc8! 21 Qxc8 ch, Rxc8 22 Nf6 ch, gxf6 23 Rxf6, Kg7 24 Raf1, Rce8 25 h4, R8e7 26 R6f4, Be4 27 Rd1, Rh5 28 a3, Ree5 29 Rdf1, f5 30 Rd1, Rh6 31 g3, c6 32 dxc6, bxc6 33 b4, d5 34 Bb3, Draw.**

CHAPTER FOUR

THE NEW MOELLER (13...h6)

(after 1 e4, e5 2 Nf3, Nc6 3 Bc4, Bc5 4 c3, Nf6 5 d4, exd4 6 cxd4, Bb4 ch 7 Nc3, Nxe4 8 0-0, Bxc3 9 d5, Bf6 10 Re1, Ne7 11 Rxe4, d6 12 Bg5, Bxg5 13 Nxg5)

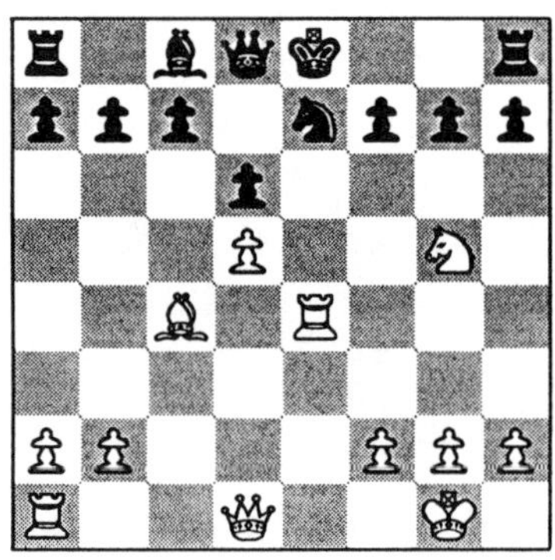

13 ... h6

This long-unappreciated move drew sudden attention after the game Barczay-Portisch, Hungarian Championship 1968-69 [see Illustrative Game (11)] in which Black forced an unsound knight sacrifice that was quickly refuted.

The immediate knight sacrifice, **13...h6 14 Nxf7!?** is questionable although it occasionally scores points, e.g. **14...Kxf7 15 Qf3 ch, Kg6?? 16 Rxe7!, Qxe7 17 Bd3 ch, Kg5 18 h4 ch, Kxh4 19 Qg3 ch, Kh5 20 Bg6** mate (Nubling-Muller, C., Correspondence 1989). Or **15...Kg8 16 Rae1!, N-moves 17 Re8 ch.**

Better is **15...Nf5!**, after which White must try to regain his piece with **16 g4**. Then his king side is weaker than Black's following **16...Rf8 17 gxf5, Kg8! or 16...g6 17 Rae1, Qf6 18 gxf5, Bxf5** (Mularcyk-Johansson, Correspondence 1985).

14 Qe2!

The strength of this move, formerly believed to lead to Black's advantage after the closing of the e-file, was only appreciated following several experiments in the early 1970's with the natural **14 Bb5 ch, Bd7 15 Qe2** (Not 15 Nxf7?, Kxf7 16 Qf3 ch, Kg8 17 Rae1 now because 17...Nf5 defends.) because of **15...Bxb5 16 Qxb5 ch, Qd7**.

The position after **16...Qd7** is a key one:

(a) **17 Rxe7 ch** fails miserably because of **17...Kxe7 18 Re1 ch, Kd8 19 Qxb7, Rc8** and Black consolidates.

(b) **17 Qxd7 ch, Kxd7 18 Nxf7?** is even worse, since **18...Rhf8!** traps the knight.

(c) **17 Qe2** as played in the Barczay-Portisch game is poor because of **17...Kf8!** followed by **...Nxd5**.

(d) **17 Qd3** is a bit better, but after **17...hxg5 18 Rae1, 0-0 19 Rxe7, Rfe8!** the attack dies and White has no compensation for his lost pawn, e.g. **20 R7e3, c5**.

(e) **17 Qxb7** is best, after which **17...0-0** leads to unclear chances that cannot be bad for Black, e.g. **18 Rae1, Ng6 19 Nf3, Rfb8 20 Qa6, Rxb2**.

14 ... hxg5

Black can insert **14...Bf5 15 Re3, hxg5 16 Re1, Be6** without significant difference. He should probably avoid **16...Kf8?! 17 Rxe7, Be6** to trap the rook because the opening of the e-file is too hot to handle.

For example, **18 Rxe6, fxe6 19 dxe6, Ke7?** (Better is 19...Qe7 20 Qf3 ch, Kg8 when 21 Qxb7, Rf8 22 Qxa7 provides White with compensation.) **20 Qg4, Qf8 21 Qxg5 ch, Qf6 22 Qb5, Rad8? 23 Qxb7, Rc8 24 Qc6, Rhd8 25 Ba6! Resigns** (Sestovach-Khresh, Zagreb 1982).

White's queenside raid in this example is a common theme in many lines of the modern Moeller because of Black's weaknesses there on light squares. This is why Black often tries to rebuild his pawn structure with ...d6-d5 and ...c7-c6 after move 17.

15 Re1

This regains the sacrificed piece and the control of the e-file should ensure a pawn's worth of compensation in lines such as **15...0-0 16 Rxe7** (e.g. 16...Bd7 17 Bd3, Re8? 18 Qh5!).

15 ... Be6!

Black correctly closes the most dangerous open line. With **15...Kf8?! 16 Rxe7, Be6** we transpose to the note to Black's 14th move.

16 dxe6

Black can keep the e-file closed now by pushing the f-pawn. Note that **16...f5?! 17 Re3, g4** (Ribas-Barajona, Chile 1990) fails to keep the kingside closed because of **18 h3**.

16 ... f6

Obviously Black cannot allow **17 exf7 ch.** Now a variety of moves have been tried for White, including the sacrificial **17 f4!?, d5 18 fxg5, Qd6! 19 Bxd5, Qxd5 20 gxf6, Qc5ch 21 Kh1, gxf6** and Black won in Cotten-Bond, U.S. Open 1991. But one move has emerged as White's best at this point:

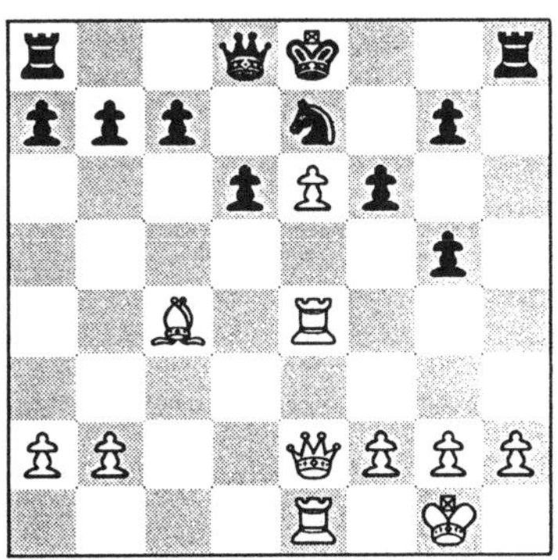

17 Re3!

This move, discovered more than 20 years ago by the American A. J. Goldsby and later attributed to the Finnish correspondence player Juhani Sorri, rehabilitates the New Moeller. White discourages king side castling because of Qh5 and Rh3. He also clears the b1-h7 diagonal for a bishop. And, if Black's king remains in the center, White will play Rh3 to force an exchange of rooks that makes Qh5 ch a mating idea. We must consider five natural responses, (a) **17...Ng6?**, (b) **17...0-0**, (c) **17...c6**, (d) **17...d5**, and (e) **17...Kf8**.

(a)

17 ... Ng6?

This natural move, preparing ...Ne5 and clearing e7 so

that Black can castle queenside, is a serious error.

18 Qc2!

Refuting Black's last move since the knight has no better move than **18...Ne7**. The reason for this is that **18...Ne5** is met by **19 Rxe5!** threatening **Qg6 ch-f7 mate**, and that the knight is attacked on other squares (18...Nf4 19 g3; 18...Nh4 19 g3; 18...Nf8 19 e7).

18 ... Ne7
19 Rh3!

This illustrates well the thinking behind Sorri's move. Black's king side becomes highly vulnerable to invasion along diagonals once the rook is exchanged off.

19 ... Rxh3

Little better is **19...Rf8 20 Rh7** or **19...Rg8 20 Bd3** (intending Bg6 ch-f7), **g6 21 Rh6 or 21 Qc3**.

20 gxh3

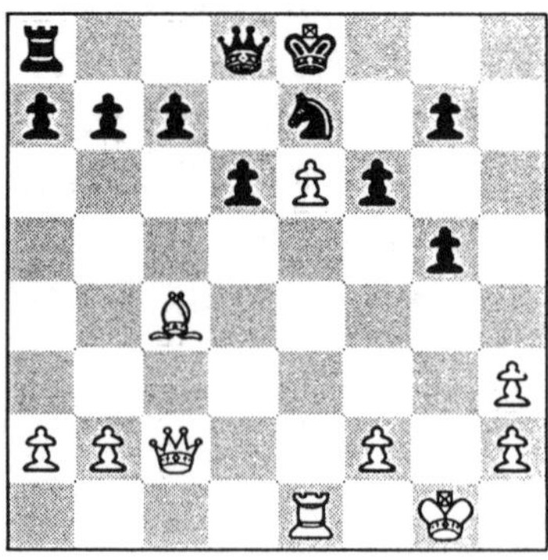

20 ... f5

Otherwise White invades with **21 Qh7!**, e.g. **20...d5? 21 Qh7** and wins.

21 Bd3

And in Sorri-Daiconescu, Correspondence 1985, White was breaking through on the king side, since **21...g6** allows **22 Qc3** and **Qh8 ch**.

Black held out for a while following **21...c6 22 Bxf5, Nxf5 23 Qxf5, Qf6** but the failure of his QR to enter the game meant that he had to play the remainder of the middlegame with a Q against Q&R. The game continued **24 Qa5, Qd8 25 Qa4, Qe7 26 Re4, d5 27 Re5, Qf6 28 Re3, d4 29 Re4, 0-0-0!? 30 Qxa7** and so on.

(b)

17 ... 0-0?

(after 1 e4, e5 2 Nf3, Nc6 3 Bc4, Bc5 4 c3, Nf6 5 d4, exd4 6 cxd4, Bb4 ch 7 Nc3, Nxe4 8 0-0, Bxc3 9 d5, Bf6 10 Re1, Ne7 11 Rxe4, d6 12 Bg5, Bxg5 13 Nxg5, h6 14 Qe2, hxg5 15 Re1, Be6 16 dxe6, f6 17 Re3)

(See diagram, next page)

This is another dubious move that should be quickly punished. Black simply does not have enough soldiers to shoot back on the king side and his king is at greater risk on g8 than at e8.

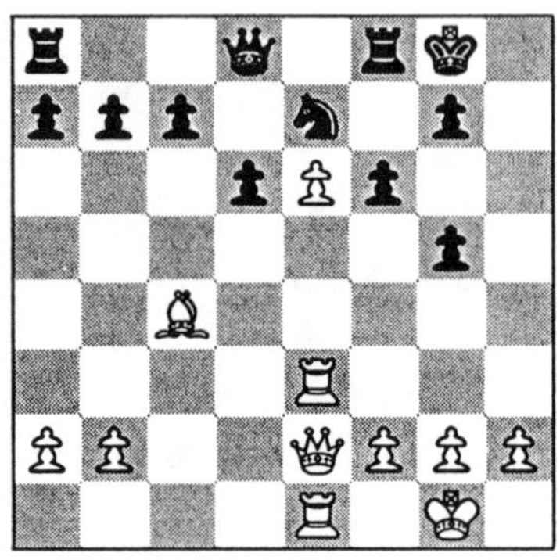

(Position after 17... 0-0)

18 Qh5

Informant analysis by the Hungarian analyst Ivan Bottlik also shows the strength of **18 Bd3,** e.g. **18...g6 19 Bxg6!, Nxg6 20 e7, Nxe7 21 Rxe7, Rf7 22 Rxf7, Kxf7 23 Qh5 ch, Kg7 24 h4!** with what Bottlik calls a winning advantage.

Note that effectiveness of h2-h4 in opening the g-file in this variation. This will be a recurring theme, particularly after White doubles his h-pawns with Rh3.

18 ... g6

White answers the natural defensive move **18...Qe8** with **19 Qf7 ch!**, winning a piece.

19 Qh6 g4

Otherwise White mates with **20 Rh3.**

20 Rh3!

Anyway. White could, in fact, announce mate in three or four moves.

20 ... gxh3
21 Re3 Nf5
22 Qxg6 ch

And Black is mated; analysis by Bottlik.

(c)

17 ... d5

(after 1 e4, e5 2 Nf3, Nc6 3 Bc4, Bc5 4 c3, Nf6 5 d4, exd4 6 cxd4, Bb4 ch 7 Nc3, Nxe4 8 0-0, Bxc3 9 d5, Bf6 10 Re1, Ne7 11 Rxe4, d6 12 Bg5, Bxg5 13 Nxg5, h6 14 Qe2, hxg5 15 Re1, Be6 16 dxe6, f6 17 Re3)

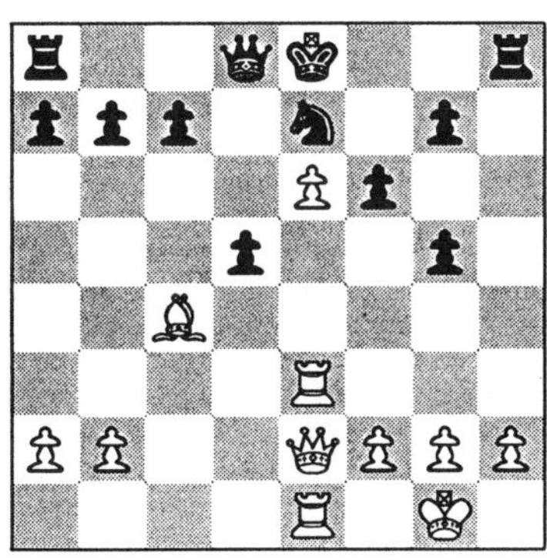

This apparently forcing move (17...d5) may permit Black to continue **18...Qd6** and **19...0-0-0**. However, White has...

18 Rh3!

Once again, this idea is dangerous. If Black retains the rook for defensive purposes (18...Rf8) he abandons control of h5. This becomes significant after **19 Bd3, Qd6 20 Qh5 ch** and then **20...Kd8 21 Qf7!**, since the Queen sacrifice cannot be accepted (21...Rxf7 22 Rh8 ch!, Ng8 23 exf7, Kd7 24 Bf5 ch, Kc6 25 Re6! and wins).

Instead, Black could try to answer **21 Qf7** with **21...Re8** but his first rank is too vulnerable and this is exploited by **22 Qxe8 ch!, Kxe8 23 Rh8 ch, Ng8 24 Rxg8 ch, Ke7 25 Rxa8** and wins (Szecsi-Heinrich, Correspondence 1986).

18 ... Rxh3

And here, **18...Ng6** runs into the familiar problem of **19 e7!** (e.g. 19...Qd6 20 Rxh8 ch, Nxh8 21 Qh5 ch, Nf7 22 Bd3, f5 — forced by the threat of the paralyzing Bg6 — 23 Bxf5, Qh6 24 Bd7 ch!, Kxd7 25 Qxf7, Re8 26 Qxd5 ch and wins — 26...Qd6 27 Qf5 ch, Kc6 28 Re6 or 26...Kc8 27 Qf5 ch, Kb8 28 Qd7, Qh8 29 Rd1).

19 gxh3

(See diagram, next page)

19 ... g6

Black cannot allow the check on h5: **19...Ng8 20 Qh5 ch, Ke7 21 Qf7 ch, Kd6 22 e7!** and Black's king cannot escape (22...Nxe7 23 Rxe7!, dxc4 24 Qe6 ch and 25 Rd7, or

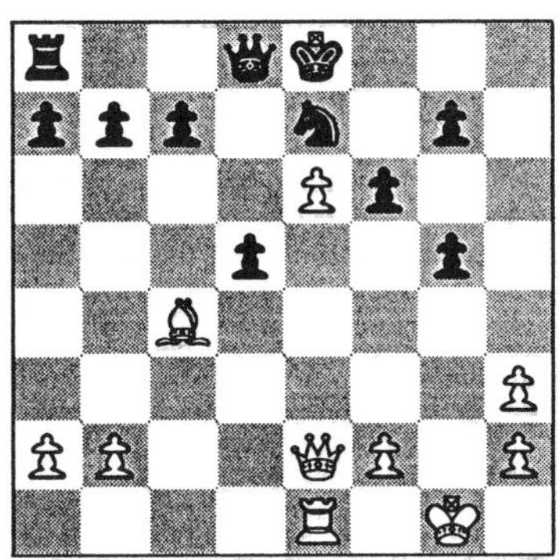

(Position after 19 gxh3)

23 Qe6 ch, Kc5 24 Bf1!, Nc6 25 Rc1 ch, Kb6 26 Qe3 ch).

Similarly **19...Kf8 20 Qh5, g6** allows **21 Qh8 ch, Ng8 22 e7 ch** and wins.

20 Qf3!

Black must now prevent the queen from capturing on f6 (20...dxc4 21 Qxf6 and wins, or 20...Qd6 21 Qxf6, 0-0-0 22 Bd3 and 23 Bxg6 with an advantage for White). But since any knight move allows Bxd5, Black must play...

20 ... f5

Surrendering the pawn with **20...Nf5 21 Bxd5, c6?** is hopeless after **22 Bxc6 ch!, bxc6 23 Qxc6 ch, Kf8 24 e7 ch!** as in a 1987 game, Janssen-Polzin.

21 Qc3! d4

And **22 Qh8 ch** could not be allowed.

22 Qb3

The forcing moves are over and Black's pawn structure has been seriously loosened. Note that White threatens not only Qxb7 but the powerful centralizing Qb5 ch - Qe5.

We are following two 1986 correspondence games by Hungarian players, both continuing **22...b6** (not 22...Qc8 23 Qb5 ch, c6 24 Qe5) **23 Qb5 ch, Kf8 24 Qe5** and now one game went **24...Ng8 25 Rd1, c5? 26 e7 ch!** and White won with a fork (26...Qxe7 27 Qd5).

The other went **24...Kg8 25 Qf6, Qf8 26 Qxg5, Rd8 27 Rd1, Rd6 28 h4, Qg7 29 Rd3** and White's heavy pieces eventually broke through (29...Kf8 30 h3, Nc6 31 Rg3, Ne5 32 h5!, Nxc4 33 h6, Qg8 34 Qf6 ch, Ke8 35 Rxg6 resigns).

(d)

17 ... c6

(after 1 e4, e5 2 Nf3, Nc6 3 Bc4, Bc5 4 c3, Nf6 5 d4, exd4 6 cxd4, Bb4 ch 7 Nc3, Nxe4 8 0-0, Bxc3 9 d5, Bf6 10 Re1, Ne7 11 Rxe4, d6 12 Bg5, Bxg5 13 Nxg5, h6 14 Qe2, hxg5 15 Re1, Be6 16 dxe6, f6 17 Re3)

(See diagram, next page)

This also gives the Black queen a way off the first rank that will facilitate ...0-0-0 — and this time the move is ...Qa5, which keeps White's queen from roaming too far from the e1 rook. The drawback to 17...c6 is that it weakens d6 slightly and is not forcing.

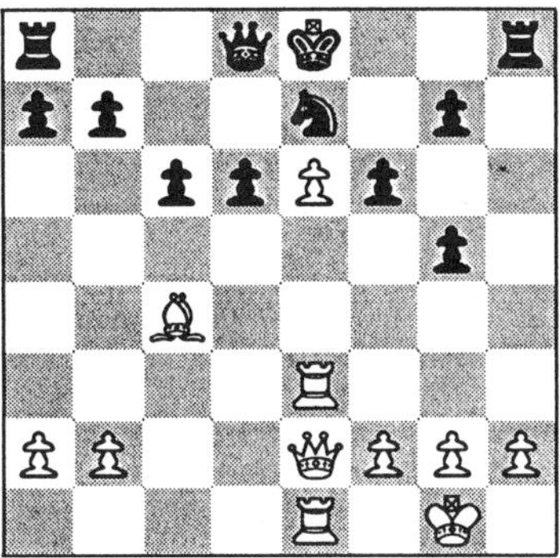

(Position after 17...c6)

18 Rh3

There is no reason to change tactics. Black has no choice now.

18	**...**	**Rxh3**
19	**gxh3**	**g6**

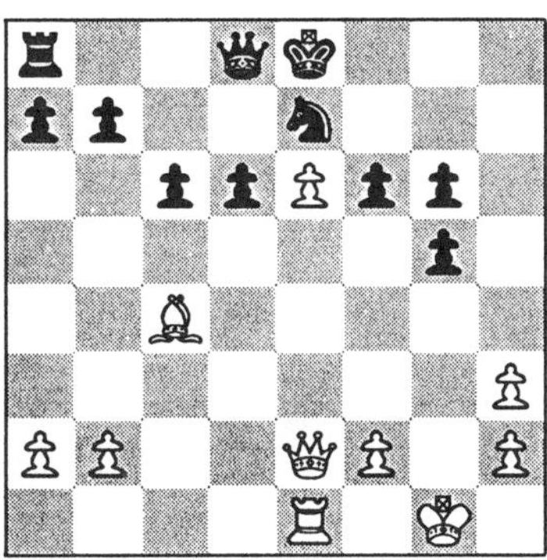

Again, the queen invasion must be averted. On **19...Qa5** White's queen becomes too powerful with **20 Qh5 ch, Kd8 21 Rd1, Qc5 22 Qh8 ch, Kc7 23 Qxg7!** (Not 23 Qxa8, Qxc4 and ...Qxe6 with compensation for the Exchange.) **d5 24 Qxf6!, Re8** (24...dxc4 25 Rd7 ch) **25 Be2** followed by **Bg4** with a clear advantage.

20 Qd2

White stops ...Qa5 with this move while preparing to attack f6 with Qc3. Black appears to be able to beat off the attack after **20 Qf3, Qa5! 21 Rd1, Qe5 or 20 Bd3, Qa5.**

And **20 b4**, with the idea of opening lines via b4-b5 while stopping ...Qa5, appears insufficient, although it worked in Illustrative Game (13), below.

New In Chess suggests a line from the Hungarian analyst E. Janosi: **20 Rd1, d5 21 h4, Qc7 22 hxg5!?, dxc4 23 gxf6, Nd5 24 Qe4, Qh7** with unclear chances. But Black has good play with the simple **21...gxh4 22 Qg4, Qc7.**

20 ... d5

On **20...Qb6** White avoids **21 Qxd6, Rd8** in favor of **21 Qc3!**.

John Nunn says **20...Kf8** with the idea of ...Kg7 before advancing the d-pawn is stronger. Since **21 h4, gxh4 22 Qh6 ch, Kg8** is unconvincing, White needs to find an improvement earlier on.

21 Qc3

Once again White offers sham sacrifice (21...dxc4? 22

Qxf6 followed by Qf7 mate or Qh8 ch) to gain ground on the kingside. Now Black has the same choice he had in the last subsection. After **21...Qc7 22 Qxf6, 0-0-0 23 Bd3** material is equal but White's pieces and passed e-pawn confer the advantage.

Better is **21...d4** when **22 Qf3, Qa5 23 Re2, Qf5** kills the initiative. But **22 Qa3** offers White some prospects. Black's queen will have to be developed, either at b6 or c7, but then castling will leave something hanging at a7 or e7. Play could continue **22...Qb6 23 Rd1, Rd8 24 Qf3.**

(e)

17 ... Kf8!?

(after 1 e4, e5 2 Nf3, Nc6 3 Bc4, Bc5 4 c3, Nf6 5 d4, exd4 6 cxd4, Bb4 ch 7 Nc3, Nxe4 8 0-0, Bxc3 9 d5, Bf6 10 Re1, Ne7 11 Rxe4, d6 12 Bg5, Bxg5 13 Nxg5, h6 14 Qe2, hxg5 15 Re1, Be6 16 dxe6, f6 17 Re3)

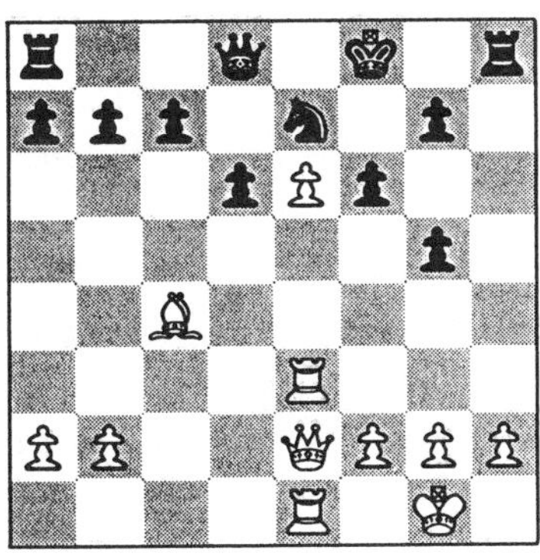

This strange move has the advantage of stopping checks at h5 while retaining the rook at h8 for defensive purposes. Black is saying, in effect, that he will begin the middlegame without connecting his rooks but by expanding in the center with ...c7-c6, ...d6-d5, ...Qd6 and ...Re8.

18 Bd3

A game Le Blancq-Williams, Wales 1988 went **18 Rh3, Rxh3 19 gxh3, g6** (19...Qe8 20 Qe4 invades at b7 or h7) **20 h4, gxh4!** (20...d5 21 hxg5!, dxc4 22 gxf6, Qd5 23 fxe7 ch, Kxe7 24 Qe3 with serious attacking — and promoting — chances for White.) **21 Qe4, Kg7 22 Qxb7, Qc8** and Black stood well. This was further tested by Videki-Petran, Ajka 1991 which went **20 Qf3!, Kg7 21 Qxb7, Qc8 22 Qf3, Rb8 23 Bb3** with chances for both sides.

But in light of the quiet nature of Black's defense, the preparatory **18 Bd3** (with Bg6-f7 in mind) is more accurate.

18 ... Kg8

Not **18...Nd5? 20 e7 ch** or **18...g6 20 Bxg6!, Nxg6 21 e7 ch** when White's rooks finally roar.

19 Qc2 Rh6

Black may not have to worry about Bg6. For example, **19...d5** (not 19...Qe8? 20 Qxc7) **20 Bg6, Nxg6** (or 20...Rh6 21 Bf7 ch, Kh8 22 Qb3 with Rh3 most in mind) **21 Qxg6, Qe8? 22 Qf5, c6 23 e7** is dangerous, but **21...Qe7!** is safe and sound.

However, on **19...d5** White's best policy may be just to use his more mobile rooks, e.g. **20 Rg3** followed by **21 Ree3** and **22 Rh3**.

21 Rg3

White prepares Ree3 and Rh3! but it appears Black can respond in time by attacking the e-pawn. Nunn gives **20...d5 21 Ree3, Qd6 22 Rh3, Rxh3 23 Rxh3, Qxe6** or **23 gxh3, Re8**.

Illustrative Games:

(11) Barczay-Portisch, Hungarian Championship 1968-69-
1 e4, e5 2 Nf3, Nc6 3 Bc4, Bc5 4 c3, Nf6 5 d4, exd4 6 cxd4, Bb4 ch 7 Nc3, Nxe4 8 0-0, Bxc3 9 d5, Bf6 10 Re1, Ne7 11 Rxe4, d6 12 Bg5, Bxg5 13 Nxg5, h6 14 Bb5 ch?, Bd7 15 Qe2, Bxb5! 16 Qxb5 ch, Qd7 17 Qe2, Kf8! 18 Nxf7 (No better is 18 Nf3, Nxd5 or 18 Qh5, Nxd5 19 Nh7 ch, Kg8!), **Kxf7 19 Re1, Ng8! 20 Re6, Kf8! 21 f4, Nf6 22 Re7, Re8! 23 Rxe8 ch, Qxe8 24 Qf2, Qh5 White resigns.** A stunning defensive accomplishment

that, at the time, seemed to refute the Moeller.

(12) Bateman-Bergraser, Correspondence 1979 —

1 e4, e5 2 Nf3, Nc6 3 Bc4, Bc5 4 c3, Nf6 5 d4, exd4 6 cxd4, Bb4 ch 7 Nc3, Nxe4 8 0-0, Bxc3 9 d5, Bf6 10 Re1, Ne7 11 Rxe4, d6 12 Bg5, Bxg5 13 Nxg5, h6 14 Qh5?!, 0-0 15 Rae1, Nf5! 16 Ne6? (Dubious, but a retreat leaves White without compensation for his sacrificed pawn.), **fxe6 17 dxe6, Qe7?** (17...Ne7! favors Black, who apparently counted on 17...Qe7 18 g4, Nh4! 19 Qxh4, Qxh4 20 e7 ch, Be6! and wins.) **18 Rf4!, c6** (The knight has no move and 18...Rf6 19 Rxf5, g6 allows 20 Qg4, Rxf5 21 Qxg6.) **19 Rxf5, Re8 20 Rf7 Resigns** — because of 20...Qg5 21 Rxg7 ch! and wins.

(13) Szecsi-Szarka, Correspondence 1987 —

1 e4, e5 2 Nf3, Nc6 3 Bc4, Bc5 4 c3, Nf6 5 d4, exd4 6 cxd4, Bb4 ch 7 Nc3, Nxe4 8 0-0, Bxc3 9 d5, Bf6 10 Re1, Ne7 11 Rxe4, d6 12 Bg5, Bxg5 13 Nxg5, h6 14 Qe2, hxg5 15 Re1, Be6 16 dxe6, f6 17 Re3, c6 18 Rh3, Rxh3 19 gxh3, g6 20 b4?, Qb6 (Now 21 b5, Kf8! 22 bxc6, bxc6 and Black gets to use the b-file rather than White, e.g. 23 h4, gxh4 24 Qd2, Qc5 or 24 Bd3, Rb8.) **21 Qb2, 0-0-0 22 b5** (This makes more sense when the enemy king is on the queenside, e.g. 22...cxb5 23 Bxb5, Rf8 24 Bd7 ch, Kd8 25 Qxb6.), **Rf8! 23 a4, Qa5?** (With 23...d5! Black stands better.) **24 Rc1, Qxa4? 25 bxc6, b6** (Now 25...Nxc6 26 Bb5, Qe4 27 Bxc6 and 28 Rb1 wins.) **26 Bb5, Qe4 27 c7, Kb7 28 Qa3, a5 29 Qxd6** and Black resigns.

CHAPTER FIVE

EUWE'S STRONG POINT VARIATION

1	**e4**	**e5**
2	**Nf3**	**Nc6**
3	**Bc4**	**Bc5**
4	**c3**	**Qe7**

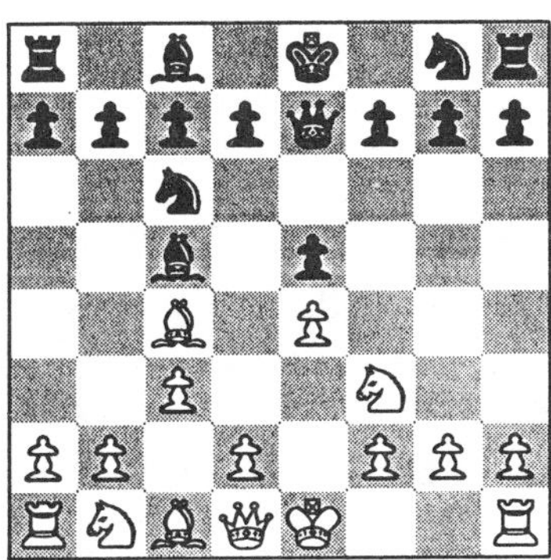

In this chapter we consider the once-popular policy of maintaining a solid Black center rather than surrendering it by ...exd4. Several masters have adopted the strong point from time to time but its most successful practitioner was Max Euwe, the world champion (1935-37) from the Netherlands.

The need for ...Qe7 to reinforce the strong point at e5 has been shown by our previous consideration of **4...d6**, since **5 d4, Bb6?** loses a pawn immediately to **6 dxe5, dxe5 7 Qxd8 ch** or **6...Qe7 7 exd6, Qxe4 ch 8 Be2** followed by **0-0** and **Re1**.

However, Black can delay the more committal queen move in favor of **4...Bb6**, and then if **5 d4**, he follows with **5...Qe7**, transposing into our main line below. For our purposes, this won't matter. (But if you're going to play the Black pieces you might prefer the bishop move, since nowadays a lot of players holding White do not intend to play a traditional Giuoco Piano, but rather a "Pseudo Ruy Lopez" with d2-d3, Nbd2 and Bb3. In that case, ...Bb6 is a useful, almost essential move but ...Qe7 may be avoidable.)

5 d4 Bb6!

The original, 16th century thinking behind **4...Qe7** was to discourage White from pushing his d-pawn because of **5 d4, exd4 6 cxd4?, Qxe4 ch** with a clean extra pawn. This opinion was discredited when the 19th century Romantics improved White's play with **6 0-0!**, offering a powerful gambit (6...dxc3 7 Nxc3, d6 8 Nd5, Qd8 9 b4!, Bb6 10 Bb2 or 8...Qd7 9 b4!, Bxb4 10 Nxb4, Nxb4 11 Qb3, Nc6 12 Bb2 with a terrific attack in either case).

Black can do a bit better by declining the gambit. He should not do it with **6...Ne5?**, a notorious trap which runs **7 Nxe5, Qxe5 8 f4!, dxc3 ch 9 Kh1, cxb2? 10 fxe5, bxa1(Q) 11 Qd5!** and wins. (Or 8 b4, Be7 9 Re1, dxc3 10 Qb3 followed by Nxc3, e.g. 10...Qh5 11 Nxc3, Nf6 12 e5, Ng4 13 h3, Nh6 14 Nd5, Bd8 15 Nf6 ch! with a winning attack, Cherbonov-Dumansky, Kharkov 1980.)

Better is **6...d3**, a common form of declining a gambit. Then **7 b4, Bb6 8 e5!** is a very dangerous attack. See Illustrative Game (14).

6 0-0 d6

Black can also play **6...Nf6** and then transpose into our line after **7 a4, a6 8 h3, d6.** There is more flexibility in move order in this kind of opening — as opposed to the Moeller Attack — because the two armies of minor pieces have yet to come into direct contact.

7 a4!

This is a useful move which could also have been inserted earlier (6 a4). The idea is to expand on the queen side — perhaps discouraging any dreams of ...0-0-0 — and creating a target for a subsequent Na3-c4. Note that the immediate threat is **8 d5** followed by **9 a5** (and if 8 d5, Na5, then 9 Bd3 followed by winning the knight with 10 b4).

White also prepares for the possible posting of a bishop at a3 and even the transfer, via a2, of his queen rook into center action.

7 ... a6

On **7...a5** Black discourages the b2-b4 advance but creates two problems for himself. He will not be able to easily keep enemy pieces off b5 now. And on a subsequent Na3-c4 the retreat ...Ba7 may end up losing the a-pawn.

A good example of what can happen is Spielmann-Shoosmith, Ostend 1907: **7...a5 8 Be3, Ba7** (to avoid the pawn-crippling 9 dxe5 and 10 Bxb6) **9 Na3, Nf6 10 Nb5!** and now Black had nothing better than **10...Bb8!?** after which **11 dxe5, dxe5 12 b4!, axb4 13 cxb4, Nxb4 14 Rcl** gave White a strong initiative. And after **14...b6 15 Nd6 ch!, Qxd6 16 Qxd6 and 17 Bd5**, a winning game.

8 h3

Although this move is ritually endorsed, it can be safely delayed or eliminated since ...Bg4 by Black is not yet a danger, e.g. **8 Na3, Nf6 9 Rel** and now **9...Bg4 10 Nc2, 0-0 11 Ne3, Bxf3 12 Qxf3, exd4 12 Nf5** with a strong attack, or **10...Bxf3 11 gxf3** followed by **Khl**. See Illustrative Game (15).

However, one of the problems with the strong-point defense is that if White takes away Black's various means of liberating his game (...Bg4, ...Nf6xe4) Black's position can become very passive. That's why the safe and sound **8 h3** has much to recommend it.

8	**...**	**Nf6**
9	**Rel**	**0-0**

Black has a problem with completing his development, since his queen bishop lacks a useful square (9...Be6? 10 d5, Na5 loses to the usual 11 Bd3! and 12 b4).

But he can still take his time about castling. On occasion, Black has tried **9...h6**. The idea is not only to stop Bg5/Na3-c2-e3-d5 or Nbd2-f1-e3-f5, but also to exploit White's eighth move with ...g7-g5-g4. When the center remains solid because of the over-protected e5 square, Black can take some liberties on the wings.

However, White can strike on the other wing more quickly: **9...h6 10 b4!** and now **10...g5 11 Ba3, g4 12 hxg4, Bxg4 13 b5** and Black has more difficulties than White.

Better is **10...0-0** but again **11 Ba3** poses problems, e.g. **11...Re8 12 b5, Na5 13 Bd3, Nd7** (otherwise 14 dxe5) **14 Nbd2, Qf6 15 Bb2, Nf8 16 Nf1** and the knight begins its advantageous climb to d5 (Markland-Stoica, Graz 1972) or **11... Nd7 12 b5, Nd8 13 Nbd2, Qf6 14 Bb2, Ne5 15 a5!** as in Keres-Berhards, Correspondence 1935.

Note that, as usual, it is extremely dangerous for Black to surrender the e5 point and/or go pawn grabbing: **9...h6 10 b4, 0-0 11 Ba3** and now **11...exd4 12 cxd4, Nxe4?** allows **13 Bd5, Bf5 14 Nbd2, Nc3 15 Rxe7, Nxd1? 16 Bxc6 or 15...Nxe7 16 Bxf7 ch, Rxf7 17 Qb3** when Black doesn't have quite enough compensation.

10 b4!

Black should stand OK after **10 Na3, Kh8!** because he can coordinate his pieces in time to meet Nd5: **11 Nc2, Ng8 12 Ne3, Ba7 13 Nd5, Qd8,** — see Illustrative Game (16).

One of the major ideas behind **10 b4** is to destroy the support for e5 and to open the vulnerable a3-f8 diagonal at the right moment. For example, routine development such as **10...Bd7 11 Ba3, Rae8** will allow **12 b5, Na5** (otherwise 13 dxe5) **13 Bd3** and the threat of **14 dxe5** is considerable.

10 ... Kh8

If he gives up the center to win a pawn with **10...exd4 11 cxd4, Nxb4** White obtains a serious edge with **12 Bg5!**, threatening **13 e5**. The point of the strange looking ...Kh8 is to reinforce the center with ...Ng8 and ...f7-f6 — making e5 a super-strong point.

In view the coming attack from b4-b5, Black can anticipate it with **10...Nd8 11 Ba3, Nd7**. However, **12 Nbd2, Qf6 13 Nf1!, Ne6 14 Ne3** retains a small edge for White (Simagin-Czerniakov, Correspondence 1948).

11 Ba3

Another idea is **11 Ra2** when the rook is heading to e2. In Speelman-Durao, London 1978, Black gave up the center with **11...exd4?** and this is usually an error in the Strong Point Variation, even when it wins a pawn — **12 a5, Ba7 13 cxd4, Nxb4 14 Rae2, Ng8 15 d5** and the threat of Ba3 led to **15...c5 16 e5, Qd8 17 e6!, Qxa5 18 Ng5, Nh6 19 exf7** and wins.

Black improves, however, with **11...Ng8.**

11 ... Ng8

This was the last chance for Black to go pawn-grabbing: **11...exd4 12 Nxd4, Nxe4** and now White will get compensation from **13 Nbd2, f5 14 b5!** and now **14...axb5 15 axb5, Nxd4 16 cxd4, Qh4!** (Not 16...Bxd4 17 Nxe4, Bxa1 because of 18 Nxd6!, Qxe1 ch 19 Qxe1, Rxa3 20 Qe7 and wins.) **17 Nxe4, fxe4.**

Here it appears Black is doing all right. But **18 Re2!**, as suggested by Euwe (in place of 18 Qd2? Ra4! or 18 Ra2, Rxa3!) offers White good chances, e.g. **18...Bxh3 19 gxh3, Rf6 20 Bxd6!.**

12 b5 Na5
13 Bd3!

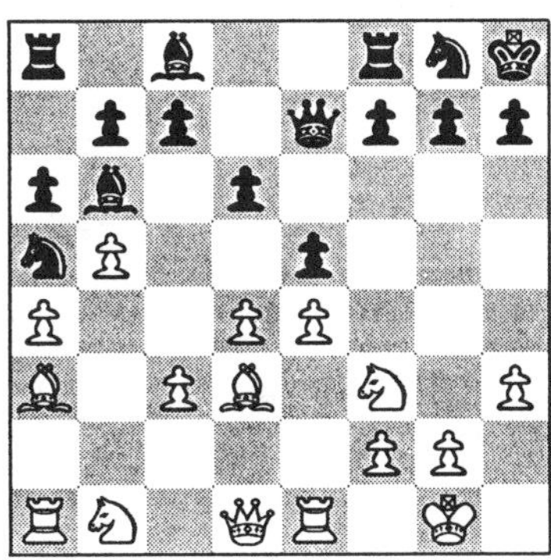

As we mentioned in chapter one, the isolation of the knight on a5 is a constant danger to Black, even though in this case there is no danger of White winning the piece. After **13...f6 14 Nbd2** White has a slight edge. The difference between the two queen knights — Black's in limbo but White's headed for d5 or f5, tells the story.

Note that **13 Nxe5?**, however, is bad: **13...f6!** and now **14 Bxg8, fxe5 15 Ba2, exd4 16 cxd4, Qf6** (Van Schelti-nga-Euwe, Maastricht 1946).

Illustrative Games:

(14) Estrin-Zhivtsov, Moscow Championship 1945 —
1 e4, e4 2 Nf3, Nc6 3 Bc4, Bc5 4 c3, Qe7 5 d4, exd4? 6 0-0, d3 7 b4, Bb6 8 e5, d6 (8...h6 is a bit better but 9 a4, a5 10 Ba3! fuels a powerful attack.) **9 Bg5, f6 10 exf6, gxf6? 11 Re1, Ne5 12 Nxe5, dxe5 13 Qh5 ch, Kd8** (Going to f8 allows 14 Rxe5!) **14 Bh4, a5 15 Rxe5!, Qf8** (15...Bg4!? 16 Rd5 ch!, Bd7 17 Nd2 is no better.) **16 Bxg8, Rxg8 17 Re8 ch!, Qxe8 18 Bxf6 ch, Qe7 19 Qd5 ch! Resigns.**

(15) Corte-Luckis, Mar del Plata 1949 —
1 e4, e5 2 Nf3, Nc6 3 Bc4, Bc5 4 c3, Qe7 5 d4, Bb6 6 0-0, Nf6 7 Re1, d6 8 a4, a6 9 Na3, Bg4 10 Nc2, 0-0 11 Ne3!, Bc8 (11...Bxf3 12 Qxf3, exd4 13 Nf5! is fine for White since g7 is now highly vulnerable to Qg3 or Bh6.) **12 Nd5!, Qd8** (12...Nxd5 13 exd5 costs a pawn.) **13 Bg5, exd4? 14 cxd4, Bg4 15 e5!, Bxf3 16 Qxf3, Nxd4 17 Qh3, dxe5 18 Bxf6, gxf6 19 Qh6 Resigns** (since Nxf6 ch cannot be averted).

(16) Contedini-Euwe, Leipzig 1960 —
1 e4, e5 2 Nf3, Nc6 3 Bc4, Bc5 4 c3, Bb6 5 d4, Qe7 6 0-0, d6 7 h3, Nf6 8 Re1, 0-0 9 a4, a6 10

Na3, Kh8 11 Nc2, Ng8 (Black's last two moves are part of a plan to support the center with the f-pawn.) **12 Ne3, Ba7**

13 Nd5? (Much better was 13 Nf5.), **Qd8 14 Be3, f6! 15 b4, Ne7 16 dxe5?** (A bad move which only gives Black the better of the two half-open files now created.), **Nxd5 17 Bxd5, Bxe3 18 Rxe3, fxe5! 19 Bb3, Qf6 20 c4?** (20 Qe2, protecting f2 and preparing Nd2, is better than this pointless advance.), **Ne7 21 c5, dxc5 22 bxc5, Ng6 23 Qd5?, Bxh3!** (A neat concluding combination.) **24 gxh3, Nh4! 25 Nxh4, Qxf2 ch 26 Kh1, Qxe3 27 Nf5?, Qxh3 ch 28 Kg1, Rf6 White resigns** in view of **29 Kf2, Rg6 30 Ne3, Qh2 ch 31 Ke1, Rg1 ch 32 Nf1, Rf8** etc.

CHAPTER SIX

INTRODUCTION
MAX LANGE

The most common way for Black to avoid the pitfalls of the Moeller Attack is simply to avoid playing **3...Bc5**. The chief alternative to the bishop move is **3...Nf6**, entering a Two Knights Defense. This can be attractive to many players since Black usually gets to play the attacking moves after **3...Nf6 4 Ng5, d5**.

However, White can seize the initiative in the Two Knights with the brainchild of Max Lange:

1	**e4**	**e5**
2	**Nf3**	**Nc6**
3	**Bc4**	**Nf6**
4	**d4**	**...**

This can involve a gambit since Black will be given the

opportunity to hold onto his pawn at d4 with a bishop at c5. Note that after **4 d4** Black has no real alternative to taking on d4.

4	**...**	**exd4**
5	**0-0**	**Bc5**

For **5...Nxe4** see Chapter Eight — Anti-Lange. The other ideas are either faulty (5...d5? 6 exd5, Na5? 7 Qe1 ch!) or passive (5...d6 6 Nxd4, Be7 7 Nc3 followed by Nf5, or 5...Be7 6 Nxd4, Nxe4? 7 Nf5!).

6	**e5**	**d5**

Black's counter in the center is considered the best, although two knight moves are still seen from time to time. One of them — **6...Ne4?** — is simply a bad move because of **7 Bd5!**. To rescue his trapped Knight Black has to go in for **7...f5**, after which **8 exf6, Nxf6 9 Bg5, Be7 10 Bxf6!, Bxf6 11 Re1 ch** leads to a quick edge, as in one of Paul Morphy's last games.

A more serious alternative for Black at move six is **6...Ng4, since 7 Bxf7 ch, Kxf7 8 Ng5 ch, Kg8 9 Qxg4** is actually in Black's favor following **9...d5!**. White does better with **7 Bf4**, threatening **8 h3, Nh6 9 Bxh6.**

This means that Black will probably meet **7 Bf4** with **7...d6**, allowing the e-file to be opened: **8 exd6, Bxd6 9 Re1 ch, Kf8** (No better is 9...Ne7 10 Bxd6, Qxd6 11 Qe2! or 9...Be7 10 Bb5, 0-0 11 Bxc6, bxc6 12 Nxd4.) **10 Bxd6 ch, Qxd6** (On 10...cxd6 White also continues 11 c3.) **11 c3** with a slight advantage to White, e.g.:

(a) **11...dxc3 12 Nxc3** with more than enough

compensation, e.g. **12...Bf5 13 Qe2** and **14 Rad1**;

(b) **11...Bf5 12 cxd4, Rd8 13 Bb5, g6 14 Bxc6, Qxc6? 15 Nc3 and Rc1** with better placed pieces (Rossolimo-O'Kelly, Trencianske-Teplice 1949); or

(c) **11...Qc5 12 Nxd4!, Nxd4** (12...Qxc4? 13 Nxc6, Qxc6? 14 Qd8 ch and mates) **13 Qxd4, Qxd4 14 cxd4, Bd7 15 Nc3** with a favorable endgame. Black has to solve his king problem before he can compete with White's rooks.

7 exf6

Not the only way of maintaining the initiative but the most aggressive. Traps start to spring up from now on.

7 ... dxc4
8 Re1 ch Be6

Black can play **8...Kf8?!** and avoid immediate disaster, but he has to be careful after **9 Bg5!**. Then **10 fxg7 ch**, winning the queen, is threatened and **9...Qd7? 10 Bh6!, gxh6 11 Qd2** is a quick way to lose the game.

Better is **9...gxf6 10 Bh6 ch, Kg8** but then **11 Nc3** sets new traps. The most obvious trap is **11...dxc3?? 12 Qxd8 ch and 13 Re8 ch mates.** Another is **11...Bg4 12 Ne4, Bb6 13 Qe2** since if Black continues with **13...Ne5** White has **14 Nxe5!, Bxd1 15 Nd7!!** with a mating attack (15...Be7 16 Nexf6 ch, Bxf6 17 Re8 ch! and 18 Nxf6). In this line Black does better with **12...Bf8 13 Bxf8, Kxf8** but his future is bleak after **14 Qd2, Kg7** (else Qh6 ch) **15 Qf4, Bxf3 16 Qg3 ch! and 17 Qxf3, or 15...Bh5 16 Nh4 and Nf5 ch.**

Another possibility after **11 Nc3** is **11...Bf5 12 Ne4, Bf8 13 Qd2!** with these consequences:

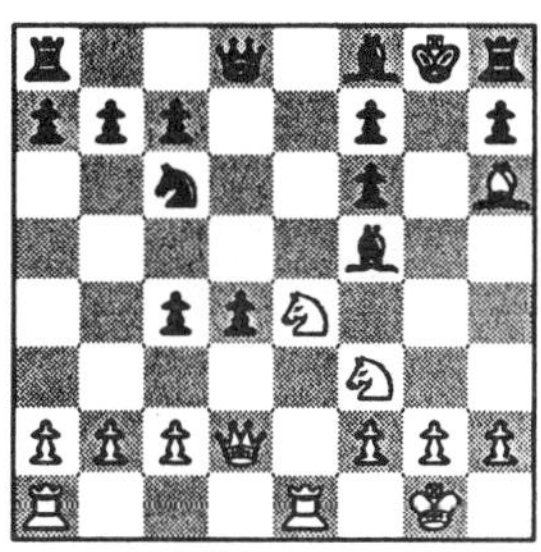

(a) **13...Bg6 14 Bxf8, Kxf8 15 Qh6 ch, Kg8 16 Nh4** with a strong attack;

(b) **13...Ne5 14 Nxd4, Bxe4 15 Rxe4, Qd5 16 Rae1** and Rautenberg-Nurnberg, Bad Pyrmont 1949 saw Black get mated via **16...Re8 17 Bxf8, Rxf8? 18 Rxe5!, fxe5 19 Qg5.**

(c) **13...Bg7 14 Ng3!** and the knight makes an impact on h5 or f5, e.g. **14...Bxh6 15 Qxh6, Bxc2? 16 Nh5;**

(d) **13...Bxh6 14 Qxh6, Bxe4 15 Rxe4, f5** and now analysis by Harding and Botterill favors White considerably with **16 Rf4, Qd5 17 Nh4, Ne7 18 Nxf5!.**

In fact, if Black can play **8...Kf8 9 Bg5, gxf6 10 Bh6 ch, Kg8** he probably must try **11 Nc3, Bf8 12 Bxf8, Kxf8 13 Ne4, f5** and see what happens after **14 Ng3.**

9 Ng5

(See diagram, next page)

The first of a series of surprising moves — surprising because White delays fxg7 because it surrenders control of e7 in lines such as **9 fxg7?, Rg8 10 Bg5, Be7!.**

The text sets one more ancient trap: On **9...Qxf6** White

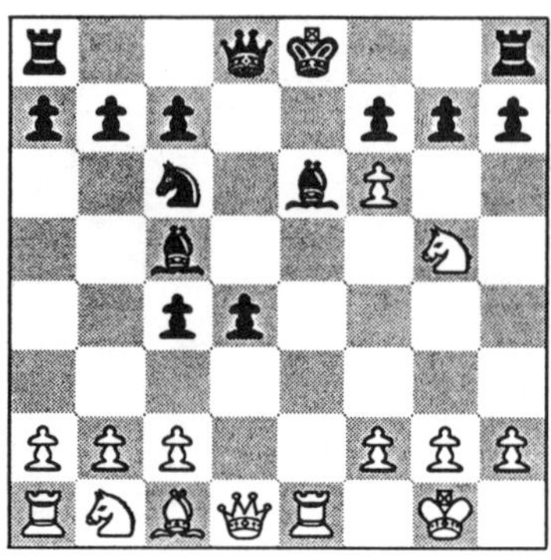

(Position after 9 Ng5)

wins with **10 Nxe6, fxe6 11 Qh5 ch and 12 Qxc5**. Black has only one convenient way of defending the e6 bishop now since **9...Qd7 10 Nxe6** allows the same Qh5 ch trick and because **9...0-0** allows **10 Rxe6!, fxe6 11 f7 ch, Kh8** (11...Rxf7 12 Nxf7, Kxf7 13 Qh5 ch) **12 Qh5, h6 13 Qg6!**.

9 ... Qd5

An idea that is either very new or very old is **9...Bf8**, with the idea of **10 Nxe6, fxe6 11 Rxe6 ch, Kf7 12 fxg7, Bxg7 13 Re1, Re8** with advantage to Black (14 Qh5 ch, Kg8 15 Rxe8, Qxe8 16 Qd5 ch, Qf7 as in Riddell-R. Levit, Chicago 1994).

10 Nc3 Qf5

Of course, not **10...dxc3?? 11 Qxd5** losing the queen! But notice how the queen becomes vulnerable on f5 to an attack by White's g-pawn.

11 Nce4

This creates a new problem for Black, since **11...Bf8,** protecting two attacked units, allows **12 Nxf7!, Kxf7** (Not 12...Bxf7 13 Nd6 ch!) **13 Ng5 ch** with a dangerous initiative whether Black retreats the king to g8 (13...Kg8 14 g4, Qg6 15 Rxe6, gxf6 16 Qf3, Kg7 17 Bf4) or to g6 (13...Kg6 14 Nxe6, gxf6? 15 g4!, Qa5 16 Bf4). In the last line Black does better with **14...Re8** but White retains chances with **15 Nf4 ch.**

11 ... 0-0-0

Still not out of trappy waters. One way to shorten the game is **11...gxf6?** which loses to **12 g4!, Qe5** (12...Qg6 13 Nxe6 and 14 Nxc5) **13 Nf3!** and the queen falls.

Black also gets into trouble after **11...Bb6** because then the long-delayed capture on g7 is dangerous: **12 fxg7, Rg8 13 g4!, Qg6 14 Nxe6, fxe6 15 Bg5!.** The combination of the bishop from g5, cutting off the king's escape, and the knight threatening to land on f6, has a great effect:

(a) **15...h6 16 Qf3!, hxg5 17 Nf6 ch, Kf7 18 Rxe6!** with a ferocious attack (18...Kxe6 19 Re1 ch, Ne5 20 Qd5 ch and wins, or 18...Rxg7 19 Rae1 and a discovered check next);

(b) **15...Rxg7 16 Qf3, e5 17 Nf6 ch, Kf7 18 h4!** and wins (Tchigorin-Teichmann, London 1899 — 18...h6 19 Ne4 ch, Ke6 20 h5, Qf7 21 Bf6!);

(c) **15...Rxg7 16 Qf3, Kd7** (Black can't afford to surrender the Exchange with 16...Rf7 17 Nf6 ch, Rxf6 — see Illustrative Game (18) **17 Nf6 ch, Kc8 18 Rxe6, Qxg5 19 h4!** and Black's queen has no good retreat (19...Qb5 20 a4, Qc5 21 Rae1, Nd8 22 Re8 with a winning attack, according to Saemisch).

In short, its more dangerous for Black to leave his king in the center than to solve the problem of his c5-bishop's vulnerability. But now his king side will be in ruins.

12 g4!

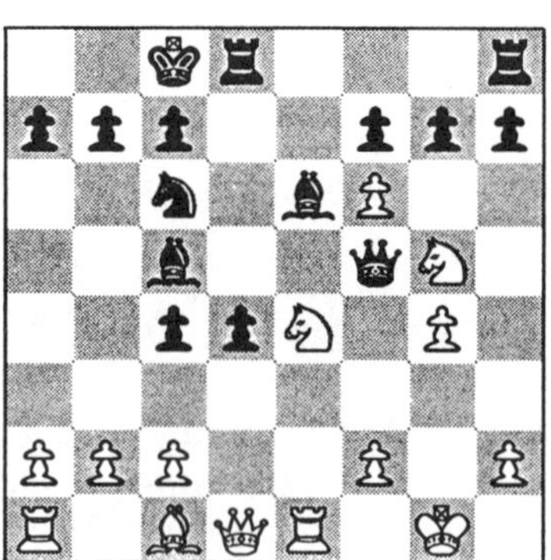

12 ... Qe5

Again **12...Qxg4** ch loses the c5 bishop. And if the queen goes to d5 it sets up a knight fork on f6 — **12...Qd5 13 Nxe6, fxe6 14 fxg7 and 15 Nf6** wins the Exchange.

13 Nxe6 fxe6

This leads to our main line discussed in the next chapter. With great luck or super knowledge Black has waded through all the traps and emerged unscathed. But the real game is just beginning.

Illustrative Games:

(17) Teichmann-Wolf, Vienna 1910 —
1 e4, e5 2 Nf3, Nc6 3 Bc4, Nf6 4 d4, exd4 5 0-0, Bc5 6 e5, d5 7 exf6, dxc4 8 Re1 ch, Kf8 9 Bg5, gxf6 10 Bh6 ch, Kg8 11 Nxd4!? (A trappy sideline based on regaining the piece with 12 c3.), **Bxd4 12 c3, Be6? 13 cxd4, Qxd4 14 Qh5, Ne5 15 Nc3, Qg4 16 Rxe5!, fxe5 17 Nd5! Resigns.** A brutal example of punishment for not knowing the main line of the Max Lange.

(18) Tchigorin & Bartolich-Tereshchenko & Shabsky, Consultation 1900 —
1 e4, e5 2 Nf3, Nc6 3 Bc4, Nf6 4 d4, exd4 5 0-0, Bc5 6 e5, d5 7 exf6, dxc4 8 Re1 ch, Be6 9 Ng5, Qd5 10 Nc3, Qf5 11 Nce4, Bb6 12 fxg7, Rg8 13 g4, Qg6 14 Nxe6, fxe6 15 Bg5!, Rxg7 16 Qf3, Rf7 17 Nf6 ch, Rxf6 (Or 17...Kf8 18 Rxe6 with a murderous attack since 18...Qxg5? 19 Nxh7 ch loses.) **18 Bxf6, Kd7**

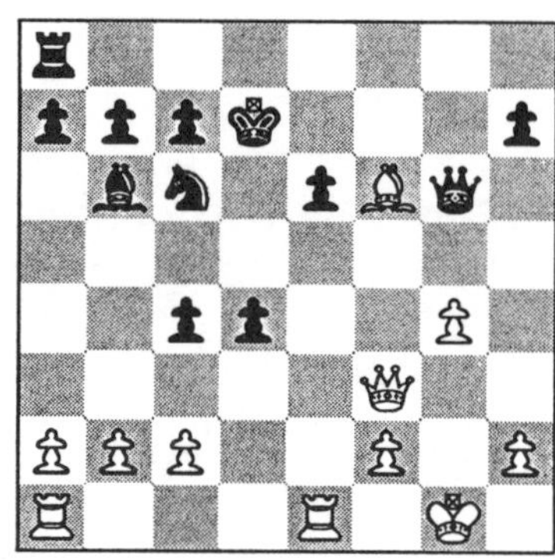

Such Exchange sacrifices by Black are not at all uncommon in the Max Lange, as we'll see in the next chapter. But here Black's central pawn mass isn't enough compensation.

19 g5, Re8 20 Qe2, Nb4 21 Red1!, d3 (Or 21...Nxc2 22 Rac1, Nb4 23 Bxd4 etc.) **22 cxd3, Nxd3 23 Rxd3 ch** (Leading to a won endgame, although 23 Rac1 should also win.), **cxd3 24 Rd1, Kc8 25 Qxd3, Qxd3 26 Rxd3, Rf8! 27 Kg2, c6 28 h4, e5 29 f3, Re8 30 h5, Re6 31 Kg3, Bd4 32 Kg4, c5** (The g-pawn decides the game faster after 32...Bxb2 33 Kf5.) **33 Kf5, Kd7 34 g6!, hxg6 35 hxg6, e4 36 Rxd4 ch!, cxd4 37 g7, Re8 38 Bxd4, Ke7** (Or 38...exf3 39 Bxa7, Ke7 40 Kg6 and wins.) **39 fxe4, Kf7 40 Bf6, b5 41 e5, a5 42 e6 ch, Kg8 43 Be5, b4 44 Kf6, a4 45 Bc7, Rc8 46 e7, Re8 47 Bd8, b3 48 a3, Kh7 49 Kf7, Rg8 50 e8(Q), Resigns.**

CHAPTER SEVEN

MAX LANGE MAIN LINE

1 e4, e5 2 Nf3, Nc6 3 Bc4, Nf6 4 d4, exd4 5 0-0, Bc5 6 e5, d5 7 exf6, dxc4 8 Re1 ch, Be6 9 Ng5, Qd5 10 Nc3, Qf5 11 Nce4, 0-0-0 12 g4, Qe5 13 Nxe6, fxe6

We left off in the following position, with White having to make his first major decision. It appears Black has weathered the opening crisis well and stands ready to exploit the weakened enemy king position or to start pushing his d-pawn.

But White is stronger on the king side than he appears at first.

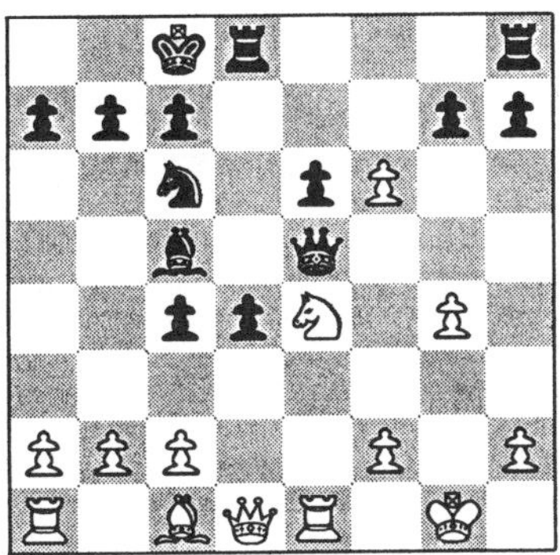

14 fxg7!

In recent years this trusty old line has been superseded by the more complex and less explored **14 Bg5**. However,

Black then has promising defenses (14...g6; 14...Bb6), based on sacrificing the Exchange to expose White's king position. The text is more forcing.

14 ... Rhg8

Of course, **14...Qxg7??** hangs the bishop at c5 one more time.

15 Bh6!

This move, introduced by Frank Marshall more than eight decades ago, turned opinions on the Max Lange upside down. Previously, White played **15 f4?** and allowed Black to expand with **15...d3 ch 16 Kf1, Qd5**. After Marshall used **15 Bh6** to win against Seigbert Tarrasch at Hamburg 1910, the theoretical tide shifted to White.

The chief value of the move is to protect the greatest asset in White's position right now — the passed g-pawn. Black is also vulnerable to a winning plan of Nf6xg8.

15 ... d3!

Black needs this advance to liberate his massed power in the center before White's king side strength begins to tell. It would appear that **15...Bb4** is an improvement on the text because **16 Re2** can then be met by the forcing **16...d3**. However, White does better with **16 f4!** (now than 16...d3 is no longer a check), and **17 Nf6**.

For example **16...Qb5 17 Nf6** and now **17...Qc5 18 Kg2!** or **17...d3 18 Nxg8** favors White. So, Black might as well go into **17...Bxe1 18 Qxe1, e5 19 Nxg8, Rxg8**. However, **20 f5!** is a winning position for White because of his passed pawns (Estrin-Chulkov, Moscow 1940).

Similarly, the endgame derived from **16...Qa5 17 Nf6, Bxe1 18 Qxe1, Qxe1 ch 19 Rxe1** is also bad for Black – **19...d3 20 cxd3, cxd3 21 f5!** as in Szirmai-Rushek, Correspondence 1946.

16 c3

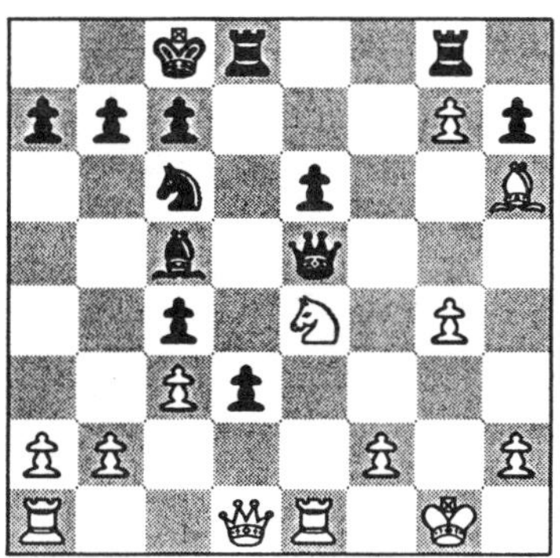

16 ... d2

This last move by Black is risky because the d-pawn will be almost certainly lost once White consolidates his position. Black is betting that he won't be able to consolidate.

Tarrasch played **16...Bd6** in the Marshall game but discovered how quickly White creates a hammerlock on the king side – **17 f4!, Qd5 18 Qf3, Be7 19 g5.** See Illustrative Game (19).

The same goes for **16...Be7**. Marshall played a short

match with Jose Capablanca to test the merits of this move [see Illustrative Game (20)] which he answered with **17. Qf3.**

But better is the direct **17 f4!, Qd5 18 Qd2.** How does Black compete against White's plan to expand on the king side? Clearly, **18...Nb8?! 19 Re3, Nd7 20 g5** doesn't work. A bit better is **18...Rd7 19 Re3, Nd8** in order to oust the bishop from h7 after ...Nf7.

However, **20 b3!, Nf7 21 bxc4** exploits the removal of minor pieces from the queen side: **21...Qxc4 22 g5 or 21...Qa5 22 Rh3, Nxh6 23 Rxh6, Rxg7** (Markelov-Ostroverkhov, Correspondence 1951-52) **24 h3!** with advantage to White.

17 Re2

White can't play Nxd2 (Bxd2, Rxg7) because of **17...Bxf2 ch! 18 Kxf2, Qxh2 ch.**

17 ... Rd3

This move has been considered best ever since another Marshall game (versus Leonhardt, San Sebastian 1911). The reason is that it is the most active move in a position that will favor White if he manages to consolidate his position with Kg2 and pushing the f-pawn one or two squares, e.g. **17...Bb6 18 Kg2!, Rd3 19 f3, Nd8 20 Rxd2** — analysis by Zemsch.

Now, after **17...Rd3**, the regrouping maneuver doesn't quite work. For example, **18 Kg2, Be3! 19 Bxe3, Qxe4 ch 20 f3, Qd5 21 Rxd2, Rxg7** and Black is better (e.g. Calton-Moody, U.S. Open 1995, 22 Rxd3, cxd3 23 Kg3, Ne5 24 Bd4, h5 25 h3, hxg4 26 hxg4, Rf7 27 f4, Ng6 28 Be3, Qe4 29 Qd2, Ne5! 30 Rf1, Nc4 White resigns).

18 Qf1!

Marshall originated this maneuver, bringing the queen to g2 and freeing d1 for his queen rook. In his game with Leonhardt Black played **18...Bb6 19 Rd1, Nd8** and managed to equalize with ...Nf7xh6. However, subsequent analysis by Olaf Ulvestad in his "Chess Charts" showed that **20 Ng3!** is strong:

(a) **20...Qf6 21 g5, Qf4 22 Qh3!** and White adds **23 g6** to his other threats. Then the d-pawn or e-pawn is bound to be lost;

(b) **20...Qd5 21 Rexd2, Nf7 22 Rxd3, cxd3 23 Rxd3** and White will remain at least a pawn up.

18	**...**	**Qd5**
19	**Rd1**	**Ne5**

Black's last two moves — another suggestion of Marshall's — were thought for many years to be the equalizer, since on **20 Nf6** he can draw with perpetual check — **20...Qf3 21 Nxg8, Qxg4 ch 22 Kh1, Qf3 ch or 22 Qg2, Qxe2.**

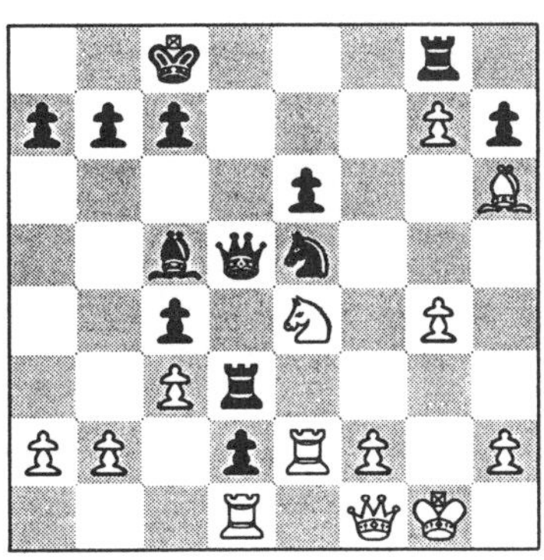

20 Qg2!

This novelty had been rejected years before because of **20...Nf3 ch 21 Kf1, Nh4 22 Qg1, Nf3** with a repetition of position. However, **23 Qg3!** avoids the draw and revives the threats of **24 Nf6 and 24 Nxc5, Qxc5 25 Re3.**

For example, **23 Qg3, Nd4** and now **23 Qf4, Nxe2 24 Kxe2, Be7 25 f3** is a promising Exchange sacrifice with threats of **26 Qf7 and 26 Nf2.** (The queen sacrifice with 24 cxd4, Rxg3 25 hxg3 is also promising.) In these positions Black is playing virtually without a rook since the one at g8 is only a sentry.

John Nunn suggests **23...Bd6 24 Nxd6 ch, cxd6** and then **25 Qf4, e5** as an improvement for Black. Then **26 Qf8 ch, Kc7** lacks point but **26 Qf5 ch** and **27 Re3** may offer better chances, e.g. **26...Kb8 27 Re3, Rxe3 28 Bxe3, Nxh2 ch 29 Ke2** or **26...Kc7 27 Re3, Rxe3 28 fxe3, Nxh2 ch 29 Kf2.**

The **20 Qg2** plan was reintroduced into play in a fairly recent game, Martinek-Vajs, Correspondence 1985 [Illustrative Game (21)]. White protects g4 and clears f1 for his king in case of ...Nf3 ch.

Note that in these lines White must be careful about pushing his g-pawn too quickly. When it advances to g5, it offers Black's queen and knight the excellent outpost square f5.

20	**...**	**Nf3 ch**
21	**Kf1**	**Be7**
22	**g5**	

And in this messy but important position, White is beginning to consolidate and make threats of Nf6 or g5-g6.

Illustrative Games:

(19) Marshall-Tarrasch, Hamburg 1910 —

1 e4, e5 2 d4, exd4 3 Nf3, Nc6 (An unusual move order but it quickly transposes.) **4 Bc4, Bc5 5 0-0, Nf6 6 e5, d5 7 exf6, dxc4 8 Re1 ch, Be6 9 Ng5, Qd5 10 Nc3, Qf5 11 Nce4, 0-0-0 12 g4, Qe5 13 Nxe6, fxe6 14 fxg7, Rhg8 15 Bh6, d3 16 c3, Bd6? 17 f4!, Qd5 18 Qf3, Be7 19 g5, Qf5 20 Ng3, Qf7 21 Qg4, Rde8?** (21...d2 is better since 22 Rxe6? allows 22...d1(Q)ch.) **22 Re4!, b5 23 a4, a6 24 axb5, axb5 25 Kg2!, Nd8 26 Qf3, Qg6**

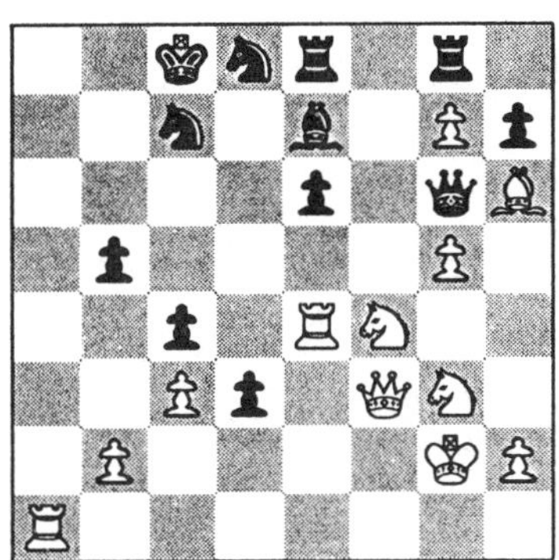

27 Rd4!, (How ironic that Black ultimately loses on the queen side.), **c6 28 Rxd8 ch!, Kxd8 29 Qxc6 Resigns**

(20) Marshall-Capablanca, New York 1910 —

1 e4, e5 2 d4, exd4 3 Nf3, Nc6 4 Bc4, Bc5 5 0-0, Nf6 6 e5, d5 7 exf6, dxc4 8 Re1 ch, Be6 9 Ng5, Qd5 10 Nc3, Qf5 11 Nce4, 0-0-0 12 Nxe6, fxe6 13 g4, Qe5 14 fxg7, Rhg8 15 Bh6, d3 16 c3, Be7 17 Qf3, Qd5 (This was the starting point in the six-game match testing this variation. Capa now tries queen side expansion.) **18 Rad1, b5 19 g5, Ne5 20 Qf4, Rd7 21 Re3!, a5 22 Rde1** (Black now has trouble meeting the opening of the e-file.), **b4 23 Nd2**

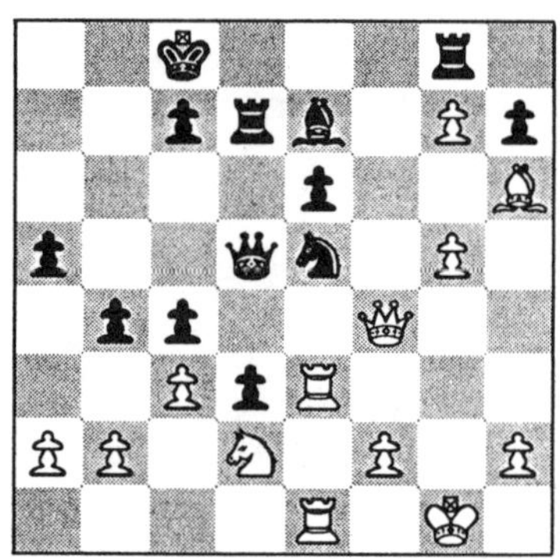

23...Bxg5!? 24 Qxg5, Nf7 25 Qh4, Nd6 (Acknowledging that he has little compensation after 25...Nxh6 26 Qxh6, Rdxg7 ch 27 Rg3.) **26 Qf6, Nf5 27 Re5!, Qb7 28 Rxf5, exf5 29 Qxf5, Qd5 30 Re5, Qf7 31 Qxf7, Rxf7 32 Rxa5, Kb7 33 cxb4, Rf6 34 Rb5 ch, Ka7 35 Rh5, Rg6 ch 36 Kf1, Rb8 37 a3, Rg8 38 Be3 ch Resigns**

(21) Martinek-Vajs, Correspondence 1985 —

1 e4, e5 2 Nf3, Nc6 3 Bc4, Nf6 4 d4, exd4 5 0-0, Bc5 6 e5, d5 7 exf6, dxc4 8 Re1 ch, Be6 9 Ng5,

Qd5 10 Nc3, Qf5 11 Nce4, 0-0-0 12 g4, Qe5 13 Nxe6, fxe6 14 fxg7, Rhg8 15 Bh6, d3 16 c3, d2 17 Re2, Rd3 18 Qf1, Qd5 19 Rd1, Ne5 20 Qg2, Nf3 ch 21 Kf1, Be7 22 g5, Qf5 23 h3, Nh4 (White was threatening to unravel with 24 Ng3!, Qg6 25 h4!, Nxh4 26 Qe4 since endgames tend to be wins for White.) **24 Ng3** (Again 24...Qg6 25 Qe4 leads to a big edge.), **Qf3 25 Qxf3, Nxf3 26 Ne4, Kd7!** (Based on 27 Nf6, Bxf6 28 gxf6, Ke8.) **27 Re3, Rxe3 28 fxe3, Ke8 29 Ke2, Nh4**

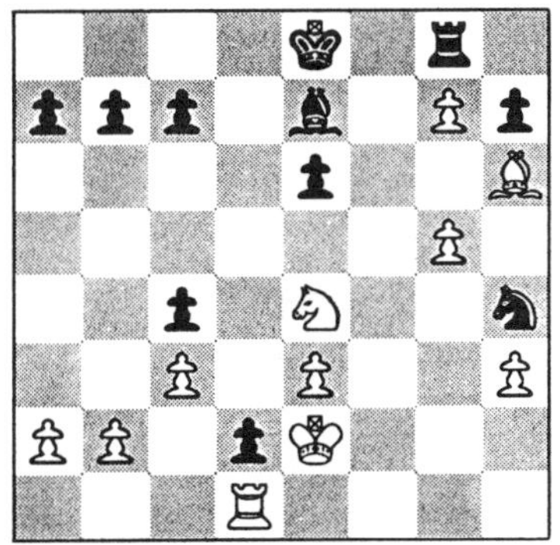

30 Nf6 ch! (Now this stroke wins.), **Bxf6 31 gxf6, Kf7 32 Bg5, Nf5 33 e4!** (The first and last move of the game, since 33...Nd6 34 Rxd2 and 35 e5 followed by Rd7 ch will decide,), **Resigns**.

CHAPTER EIGHT

THE ANTI-MAX LANGE VARIATION

You may be wondering why, if the Max Lange is theoretically sound, you don't see it being played in grandmaster games. The answer is that Black usually avoids it nowadays by way of the following:

1	**e4**	**e5**
2	**Nf3**	**Nc6**
3	**Bc4**	**Nf6**
4	**d4**	**exd4**
5	**0-0**	**Nxe4**

This leads to another highly theoretical variation, one that has been analyzed so thoroughly that to reach a new conclusion — that White, in fact, can achieve a significant advantage — requires analyzing matters well beyond what we would normally call the opening. In fact, as the following analysis shows, we cannot reach a clear conclusion before a king-and-pawn endgame at the 28th move!

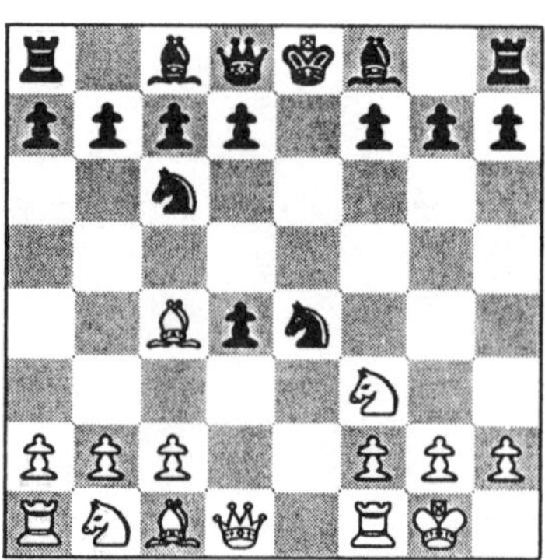

At first Black's last move looks too risky because of the e-file pin that ensues. However, Black will be able to support his center with **6...d5.**

6 Re1 d5

Clearly, Black cannot rely on the other pawn (6...f5 7 Nxd4, Bc5? 8 Rxe4 ch, fxe4 9 Qh5 ch or 7...d5 8 Bb5 and f2-f3) or the tactics of **6...Be7 7 Rxe4, d5** because White remains materially ahead after **8 Rxe7 ch.**

7 Bxd5! Qxd5
8 Nc3 ...

A remarkable position: White uses two pins to regain his sacrificed bishop. Black now has five reasonable-looking moves for his attacked queen. Two of them, however, are grossly inferior — **8...Qc4 9 Nd2!, Qa6** (9...Qc5 10 Ndxe4) **10 Nd5, Qa5 11 c4, Be6** (11...dxc3 12 Nc4!) **12 Nb3** or **8...Qf5 9 Nxe4, Be6 10 Nxd4, Nxd4 11 Qxd4, Be7!? 12 Bh6!.**

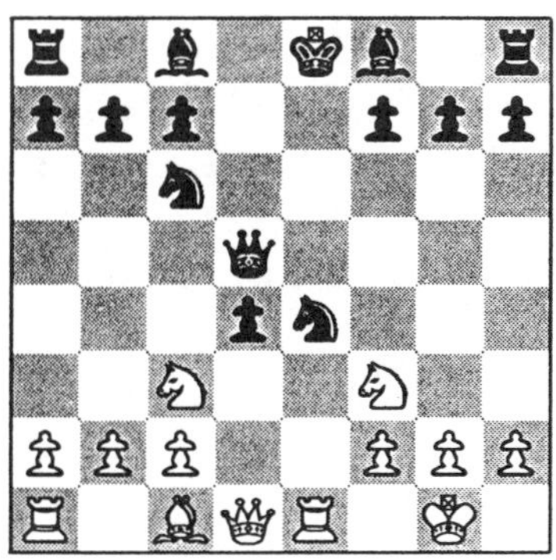

8 ... Qa5!

This prevents White from regaining his pawn as in the last line of the last note because **9 Nxe4, Be6 10 Nxd4, Nxd4 11 Qxd4** would now allow **11...Qxe1 mate.**

Black needs to castle quickly in these positions and this explains why **8...Qd8** is inferior: **9 Rxe4 ch!, Be6 10 Nxd4** gives White too long-lasting an initiative. See Illustrative Game (22). Also note that **9...Be7** (rather than 9...Be6) is poor after **10 Nxd4** because the attempt to embarrass the rook with **10...f5** runs into a questionable endgame after **11 Rf4, 0-0 12 Nxc6, Qxd1 ch 13 Nxd1, bxc6 14 Ra4.**

We should also mention the fifth and final queen move: **8...Qh5**. It is not at all bad. Its chief drawback is that the queen might turn out to be trapped on the king side after **9 Nxe4, Be6 10 Bg5!, e.g. 10...Bb4 11 c3, dxc3 12 bxc3, Ba5 13 h4!**, threatening **14 Ng3, Qg4 15 Re4 or 14...Qg6 15 h5** (but 13...Qg4 14 Ng3, Bb6 15 Rb1, Qc4 may hold).

If Black avoids **10...Bb4** in that variation, he gets a bad endgame from **10...Be7 11 Bxe7, Nxe7 12 Nxd4, Qxd1 13 Raxd1, 0-0-0 14 Ng5** and a dubious middlegame from **10...h6 11 Bf6!, Qa5 12 Nxd4!, e.g. 12...gxf6 13 Nxf6 ch, Ke7 14 b4!, Nxb4 15 Nxe6!, Kxf6 16 Qd4 ch, Kg6 17 Qxh8, Nxc2 18 Nxf8 ch** (Rossolimo-Prins, Bilbao 1951).

One rare line, not mentioned in Botterill & Harding, is **10...Bd6** which allows Black to meet **11 Bf6** with **11...0-0!** and rough equality after **12 Nxd6 and 13 Bxd4.** White does better with **11 Nxd6 ch, cxd6 12 Bf4, 0-0 13 Nxd4.**

9 Nxe4 Be6

Black needs to castle but if he tries to do it on the king side (9...Be7 10 Bg5, 0-0 11 Bxe7, Nxe7 12 Nxd4) White emerges with too much centralized strength. After **9...Be6** Black at least gets some serious counterplay because of his entrenched d-pawn and the extra space that confers on him.

10 Neg5

Botterill and Harding in their 1977 Batsford book on the Giuoco say of this: "Not a bad move, but unfortunately everybody nowadays seems to know how to meet it!"

That conclusion seems a bit overly generous, as we'll see.

10 ... 0-0-0

Trying to hold onto the extra pawn is clearly foolhardy (10...Qd5 11 Nxf7).

11 Nxe6 fxe6
12 Rxe6

Now **12...Bc5** is clumsy because it locks in the queen and sets up a possible pawn fork at b4 later on.

(See diagram, next page)

Also possible is **12...Qf5**, preparing to push the d-pawn, e.g. **13 Qe2, Bc5 14 Bg5, d3**. Now Kemp-Harding, Correspondence 1973, led to a rapid exhaustion of fighting force with **15 cxd3, Rxd3 16 Re1, h6** (16...Rxf3? 17 Re8 ch) **17 Re8 ch?, Rxe8 ch 18 Qxe8 ch, Nd8.**

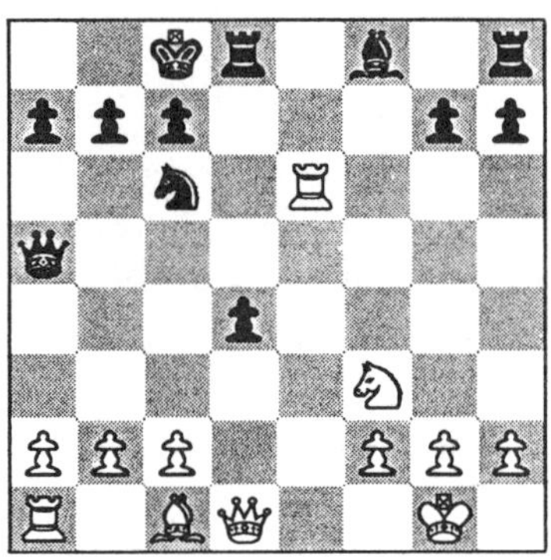

(Position after 12 Rxe6)

But in these positions in which White posts a bishop at g5 he is quite willing to retreat it to g3, e.g. **17 Bh4, g5 18 Bg3** and now **18...Rhd8? 19 Rxh6** or **18...h5 19 Rxc6, cxd6 20 Ne5.**

Instead of pushing his d-pawn at move 14 Black can play **14...Rdf8** as in our main line below. A good example of play for White is Illustrative Game (23).

A final **12...Qf5** sequence for Black, recommended by Bogolyubov, runs **13 Qe2, h6** stopping the White bishop from reaching its useful g5 post. The crucial line then is **14 Bd2, Qxc2 15 Rc1, Qxb2** and now **16 Rexc6!, bxc6 17 Qe6 ch, Kb8 18 Ne5.** Black may hold but it's not clear how. Similarly, **18 Qe4, d3 19 Ne5** as in Gunther-Schmidt, correspondence 1988, which went **19...Ka8 20 Nxc6, Qb7 21 Qa4, Bd6 22 Rc3, Qb1 ch 23 Bc1** and won.

12 ... Bd6

To discourage White's next move Black has also tried **12...h6** but this will likely transpose into the previous note after **13 Qe2**, since Black's best reply is probably **13...Qf5**. On the other hand, **13...Bd6**, as in Djurhuus-Blees, Gausdal 1993, looks fine for Black after **14 h3?!, Qf5 15 a3?!, Kd7 16 Re4, Rde8**. But White can improve with either **14 Qe4** or **15 Re4**.

13 Bg5

Not just developing a piece with tempo, this move also seeks to reposition the bishop, as mentioned earlier, at g3.

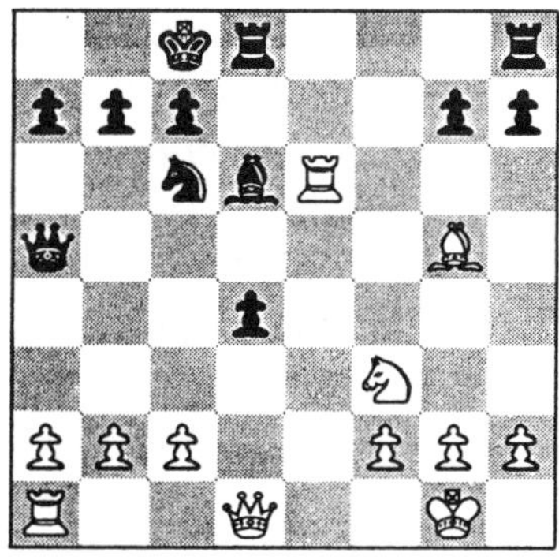

13 ... Rde8

At one time, shifting the rook to f8 was considered stronger because of a possible rook capture on f3: **13...Rdf8 14 Qe2, Kd7** (Not yet 14...Rxf3 because of 15 Re8 ch.) **15 Re1, Rxf3 and now 16 Bd2?, Qh5 17 Qxf3, Bxh2 ch!.**

However, subsequent analysis demonstrated that White can sacrifice back soundly with **16 Qxf3!, Qxg5 17 Qf7 ch:**

(a) **17...Kc8 18 Re8 ch, Rxe8 19 Rxe8 ch, Nd8 20 Qe6 ch, Kb8 21 f4!!, Bxf4 22 Qd7** and White wins; analysis by Estrin;

(b) **17...Ne7 18 f4, Qc5 19 Rxe7 ch!, Bxe7 20 Re5, Qd6 21 Rd5** or **20...Qb6 21 Rxe7 ch** and wins (Sundquist-Gabran, correspondence 1973-74).

(c) **17...Be7 18 f4, Qc5 19 R6e5!, Nxe5 20 Rxe5** and wins.

Note that if Black avoids the Exchange sacrifice, he also runs into problems after **15...d3 16 Qxd3!, h6 17 Bh4.** Also the delayed sacrifice — **15...d3 16 Qxd3!, Rxf3 17 Qxf3, Qxg5 18 Qf7 ch, Be7** — is based on the finesse that now **19 f4** fails to **19...Qc5** with check.

But the extra pawn in this line means White can play the game quietly with **19 b4!** and a queen side advance that should leave Black defenseless (19...a6 20 c4, Kd8 21 f4, Qg4 22 Rxc6! — Fagerstrom-Rosenberg, correspondence 1973-74).

One unresolved question here is whether Black can tempt fate at move 15 with **15...Qxa2!?** and then **16 Qe4, Qa5 17 Re8, Qxe1 ch!** (instead of 17...Rxe8?? 18 Qg4 ch). In a 1987 game Black had reasonable chances after **18 Nxe1, Rxe8 19 Qf5 ch, Re6 20 Qf7 ch, Ne7 21 Nd3, c5** but perhaps **22 f4**, intending **23 f5** and **Qxg7** offers White prospects for future improvement.

14 Qe1

Given a question mark — but no explanation of why — in the 1977 Batsford book. Apparently the authors thought that the endgame favors Black. We'll see.

The old idea was **14 Qe2** but after **14...Kd7 15 Rae1?, Qxe1 ch!** Black stands, if anything, a little better. White *can* play **14 Qe2** for a win if he is willing to meet **14...Kd7** with **15 Rxe8, Rxe8 16 Qd3** as in Pozin-A. Popov, Russia 1993 and some earlier games. He appears to have a slight edge.

14	**...**	**Qxe1 ch**
15	**Raxe1**	**Rxe6**
16	**Rxe6**	**Kd7**

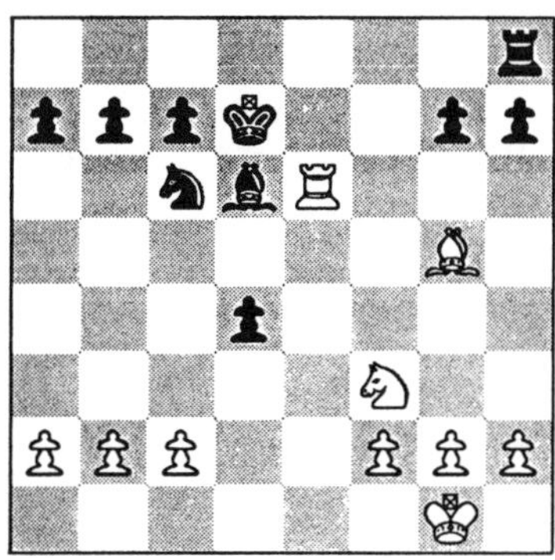

This kind of position, resulting from other variations, has been rated as equal and can even be judged as favorable for Black, in view of his queen side pawn majority and because his king will be more centralized, at d5, after the impending exchange of rooks.

However, the d4-pawn is as more of a weakness than a source of strength. White, meanwhile, threatens to centralize his king at d3. To stop that, Black's natural policy is an exchange of the last pair of rooks.

17 Re4 Re8

Inserting **17...h6 18 Bd2!** at this point, or a move earlier or later, will make little difference.

18 Rxe8 Kxe8
19 Kf1

In some older games White played indifferently, e.g. **19 a4?** and got into trouble because his king was too far away (19...Kd7 20 Bd2, Be7 21 Kf1, Bf6 22 Ke2, Ke6 23 Bf4, Bd8 24 Bg5, Kd5 25 Bd2, Bf6 26 Kd3, a6 27 c3, dxc3 28 bxc3, Na5 29 Ng5, Bxg5! 30 Bxg5, Nc4 31 Kc2, c6 32 h4, h5 33 f3, b5 etc., as in Lagland-Sarink, correspondence 1980).

19 ... Kf7
20 Bd2 h6

Not **20...Ke6 21 Ng5 ch.** It may seem that we have extended this "opening" analysis far beyond its natural limits. But this is one of those instances in which the correctness of Black's decisions around move 12 or 13 — important decisions for an evaluation of the Two Knights Defense — must be carried out to their logical conclusion. If, in fact, Black is equal in the next few moves, then **13 Bg5** has been a failure for White.

21 Ke2 Ke6
22 Kd3 Kd5

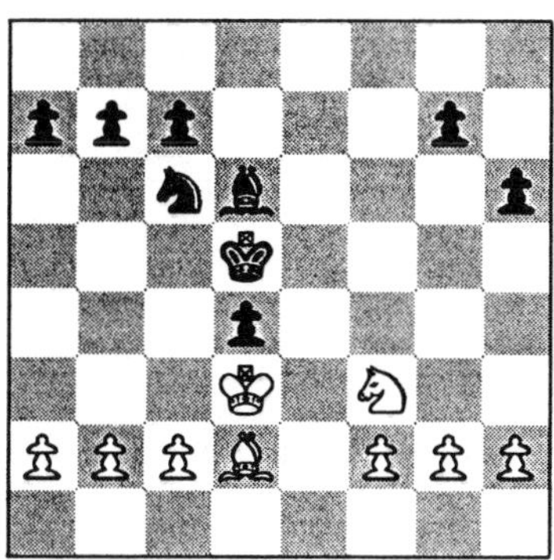

23 Nxd4!

On this trick (23...Nxd4 24 c4 ch regains the piece at a pawn profit) the proper evaluation of Black's play for the past 10 moves turns. In the key game Isaev-Gordon, World Correspondence Championship 1988-89, White converted his temporary material advantage simply: **23...Nxd4 24 c4 ch, Ke5 25 f4 ch, Kf5** (Otherwise Black remains just a pawn down.) **26 Kxd4, Bxf4 27 Bxf4, Kxf4 28 b4!**.

Now Black can lengthen the game with **28...h5**, although White should win the resulting queen-and-pawn endgame after **29 Kd5, Ke3 30 c5, Kf2 32 Ke6.**

In the game, White won the pawn endgame because he can force an inroad on the queen side before Black can create one on the king side. **28...Kf5 29 Kd5, Kf6 30 a4, Ke7 31 a5, Kd7 32 g4, Ke7 33 a6! Resigns.**

Going back to the diagram, we have to deal with Bisguier's **23...Ne5 ch 24 Kc3, Ng4** which we saw in the introduction. Instead of **25 Be3?** White keeps his edge with **25 f3**, e.g. **25...Nxh2 26 Kd3** followed by **27 Nf5, 27 Nb5** or **27 c4 ch**, or **25...Be5 26 fxg4, Bxd4 ch 27 Kb3, Ke4 28 c3.**

Illustrative Games:

(22) Tringov-Rossetto, Amsterdam 1964 —

1 e4, e5 2 Nf3, Nc6 3 Bc4, Nf6 4 d4, exd4 5 0-0, Nxe4 6 Re1, d5 7 Bxd5, Qxd5 8 Nc3, Qd8 9 Rxe4 ch (9 Nxe4 allows Black to castle quietly after 9...Be7), **Be6 10 Nxd4, Nxd4 11 Rxd4, Qc8 12 Bg5, Bd6 13 Ne4** (Black now decides to offer a pawn...)

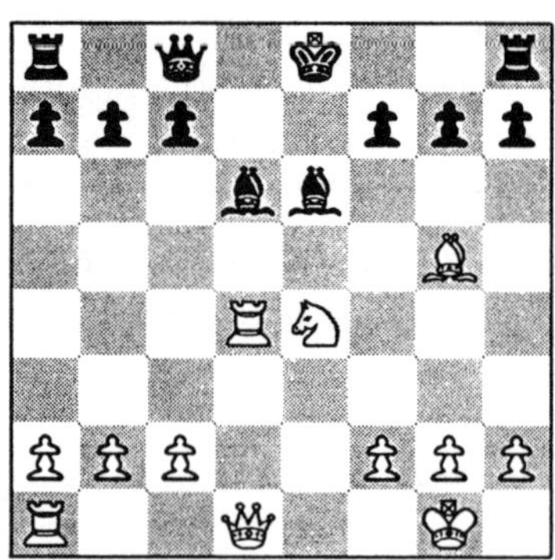

13...0-0? 14 Nf6 ch!, gxf6 15 Bxf6, Rd8 (15...Be5 16 Bxe5, f6 keeps the game going) **16 Qh5, Kf8 17 Qxh7, Ke8 18 Rad1 Resigns** (Black is terminally tied up.).

(23) Bielczyk-Przewoznik, Polish Championship 1981 —

1 e4, e5 2 Nf3, Nc6 3 Bc4, Nf6 4 d4, exd4 5 0-

0, Nxe4 6 Re1, d5 7 Bxd5, Qxd5 8 Nc3, Qa5 9 Nxe4, Be6 10 Neg5, 0-0-0 11 Nxe6, fxe6 12 Rxe6, Qf5 13 Qe2, Bc5 14 Bg5, Rdf8 15 Re1, Qd5 16 a3, a6 (Black creates luft and anticipates b2-b4-b5.) **17 Bh4, Kb8 18 Qd3, g5?** (A pawn sacrifice based on 19 Bxg5, Rxf3 or 19 Nxg5, Rhg8 with chances on the file.) **19 c4!, Qd8 20 Nxg5, h6 21 Nf3, Qd7 22 b4, Bd6 23 Bg3!** (Effectively killing the attack.), **Bxg3 24 hxg3, Rd8 25 R6e4, Qf5 26 b5, Na7 27 bxa6, b6 28 Ne5, Rhe8 29 g4, Qh7 30 Qg3, Re7 31 c5!, d3** (Desperation.) **32 cxb6, d2 33 bxa7 ch, Ka8 34 Qf3!, dxe1(Q) ch 35 Rxe1 ch, c6 36 Qxc6 ch, Kxa7 37 Qc5 ch, Ka8 38 Rc1, Qe4 39 Qxe7 Resigns.**

(24) L. Roos-Ernst, Copenhagen 1981 —

1 e4, e5 2 Nf3, Nc6 3 Bc4, Nf6 4 d4, exd4 5 0-0, Nxe4 6 Re1, d5 7 Bxd5, Qxd5 8 Nc3, Qa5 9 Nxe4, Be6 10 Neg5, 0-0-0 11 Nxe6, fxe6 12 Rxe6, Bd6 13 Bg5, Rdf8 14 Qe2, h6 15 Bh4, Qb4 16 Rb1, a5 17 Re4! (White goes after the d-pawn now, beginning with the threat of 18 c3.) **Qc5 18 Rd1, g5 19 Bg3, Bxg3 20 hxg3, Rd8 21 Ne5, Nxe5 22 Rxe5, Qb4? 23 Rb5, Qa4?** (He had to surrender the a-pawn.) **24 Qe6 ch, Kb8 25 Qc6 Resigns** (In view of 25...b6 26 Rxb6 ch.).

CHAPTER NINE

OTHER GIUOCO DEFENSES

Last — and, in effectiveness, least — are the other third moves available to Black. They are, in general, either overly passive or overly risky.

If passive, White should respond with a quick advance of his d-pawn. The correct replies to the risky third moves virtually suggest themselves.

1	**e4**	**e5**
2	**Nf3**	**Nc6**
3	**Bc4**	

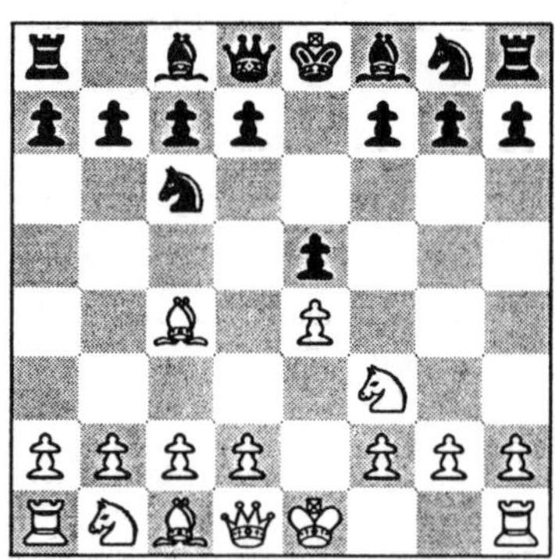

The remaining moves at Black's disposal will be disposed of in the following sections: (a) **3...Be7**, the Hungarian Defense; (b) **3...d6**, sometimes known as Alekhine's Variation; (c) **3...g6**, the rare fianchetto defense; (d) **3...Qf6?**; (e) **3...f5?**; (f) **3...Nd4?**.

Other moves are met more powerfully by **4 d4!** (or 3...Nge7 by 4 Ng5!). For example, **3...h6?**, designed to stop Ng5, White has **4 d4, exd4 5 Nxd4** with advantage in development and in center strength.

(a)

The Hungarian Defense, **3...Be7**
(after 1 e4, e5 2 Nf3, Nc6 3 Bc4)

This modest system allows Black to play a kind of Philidor's Defense with his queen knight more actively placed at c6, rather than d7. However, Black lacks maneuvering room and that may deny him active counterplay.

4 d4

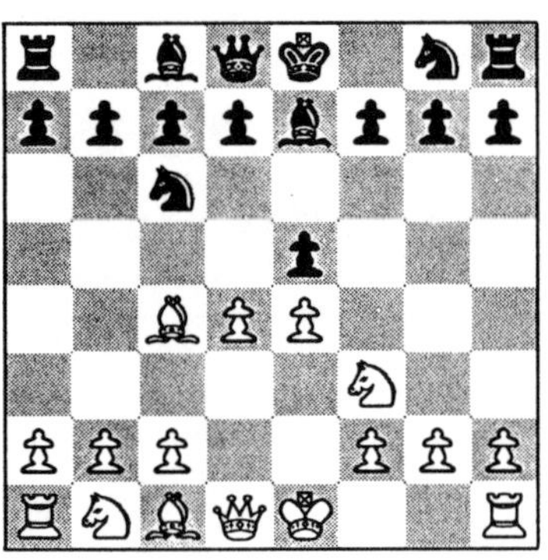

4 ... d6

Compared with the Philidor's, here **4...exd4** is not particularly bad because White's e-pawn will come under fire after **5 Nxd4, d6 6 0-0, Nf6 7 Nc3, 0-0** and **...Re8.**

It's a matter of taste, but we prefer meeting **4...exd4** with **5 c3.** This looks like a gambit, but if Black plays **5...dxc3?** he invites **6 Qd5!, Nh6** (Forced.) **7 Bxh6, 0-0.** Then Black regains his piece (8 Bc1?, Nb4 9 Qd1, c2!). But either **8 Bxg7** or **8 Nxc3** confers an edge on White.

Similarly, the typical method of declining a gambit with **5...d3** is also questionable here because of **6 Qb3!**, e.g. **6...Na5 7 Bxf7 ch, Kf8 8 Qa4, Kxf7 9 Qxa5** and White is better because of the troubled enemy king (Karaklaic-Knezhevic, Yugoslavian Championship 1977 went 9...c6 10 Ne5 ch, Ke6? 11 Nxc6! won at least one pawn because of the threat of Qf5 mate.).

Black may have to answer **5 c3** with **5...Nf6 6 e5, Ne4** (Now 6...d5 fails to 7 exf6, dxc4 8 fxe7!) **7 Bd5, Nc5 8 cxd4, Ne6** (Evans) which is barely playable for Black. Also possible, but ugly, is Tchigorin's **5...Na5** when **6 Qxd4, Nxc4 7 Qxc4, Nf6 8 e5, d5** does well but **6 Bd3**, continuing in true gambit style, looks preferable.

5 dxe5

The simplest way of dealing with Black's system. Although it frees Black's game a bit his problems continue due to White's dominance of the d-file.

5 ... dxe5

Not **5...Nxe5? 6 Nxe5, dxe5** because of **7 Qh5!**, hitting both f7 and e5.

6 Qxd8 ch Bxd8
7 Nc3 Nf6

With **7...f6** Black solves the problem of his e-pawn but creates a monster out of the bishop with the great c4-g8 diagonal. True, Black threatens to drive the White bishop off his favorite line with **8...Na5**. Therefore, **8 a3** would be correct, after which **8...Na5 9 Ba2, b6 10 Be3, Nb7 11 0-0-0!, Nd6 12 Nd2** and **Nc4** gave White a clear advantage in Rossolimo-Euwe, Beverwijk 1953.

8 Be3

Keres recommends **8 Bb5**, which also leads to a slight edge. But the text, which aims at discouraging castling, is more natural.

8 ... 0-0

The transfer of **8...Nd7 9 0-0-0, Nb6** merely encourages **10 Bb5, f6 11 a4!**; see illustrative game 23. Perhaps **8...Be7** makes this line playable, although **9 0-0-0, 0-0 10 Nd5 or 10 Nb5** offers reason to doubt it.

9 Bc5 Re8

Interposing on e7 loses the e-pawn.

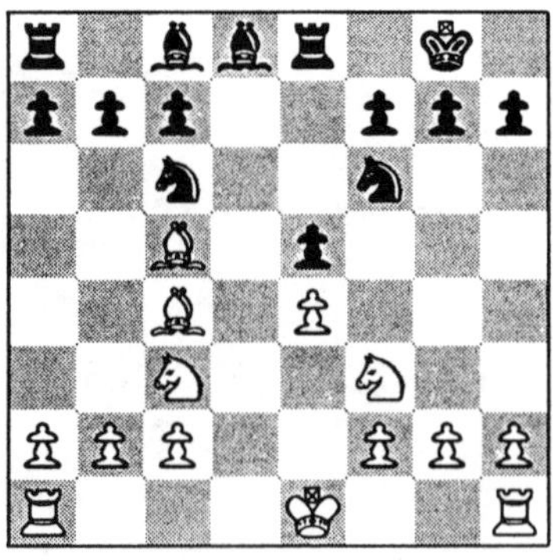

10	**Ng5!**	**Be6**
11	**Nxe6**	**fxe6**
12	**Bb5!**	

By preventing **12...Nd4**, White retains an obvious positional edge. Now in Vasiukov-Gheorghiu, Manila 1974 Black tried **12...Nd7** but stood badly after **13 Bxc6, bxc6 14 Ba3, Nb6 15 b3, Be7 16 Bxe7, Rxe7 17 0-0-0.**

In a later game, Estrin-Tichy, Prague 1985, Black played the immediate **12...Be7** but also got the worst of it after **13 Bxe7, Rxe7 14. Bxc6, bxc6.**

(b)

Alekhine's Variation, **3...d6**
(after 1 e4, e5 2 Nf3, Nc6 3 Bc4)

This early favorite of Alexander Alekhine's prepares to exert pressure on the center with ...Bg4 in connection with either ...Qe7 and ...g6 or ...Qf6 and ...0-0-0.

4 c3

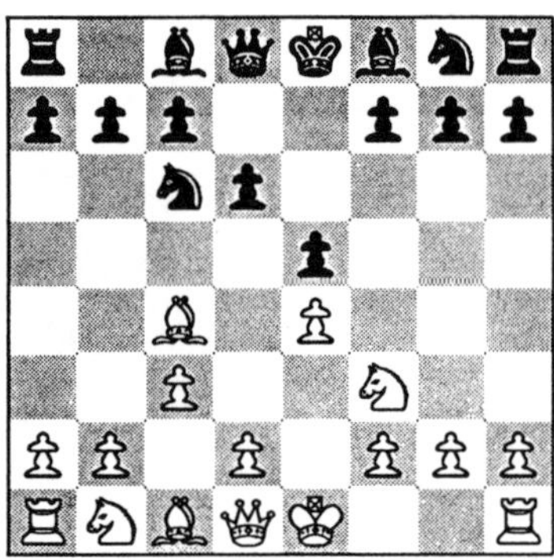

There is nothing wrong with **4 d4**, since **4...exd4 5 Nxd4** will likely transpose to the Hungarian Defense, see note to Black's 4th move in section (a) above.

With **4 c3**, however, White prepares to keep two pawns in the center and enables himself to strike quickly at f7 with Qb3. For example, **4...Nf6?** walks into **5 Qb3, Qd7 6 Ng5**. Black can try to neutralize the bishop with **4...Be6 5 Bxe6, fxe6** as Tartakower used to play, but then **6 Qb3** followed **7 Ng5** and **8 0-0** are certain to provide at least a small edge.

4 ... Qe7

On **4...Bg4** White can play adventurously with **5 Qb3!?, Qd7 6 Bxf7 ch, Qxf7 7 Qxb7** or conservatively with **5 d3** (E.g. 5...Qd7 6 h3, Be6 7 Nbd2, Nf6 8 0-0, Be7 9 Re1, 0-0 10 Bb5, a6 11 Ba4 with a favorable version of a Ruy Lopez — Malevinsky-Lutikov, Sverdlovsk 1985.).

But there is no reason to avoid the intended **5 d4, Qe7 6 Be3,** since it is hard to imagine Black going pawn-grabbing (6...exd4 7 cxd4, Qxe4 8 Nc3, Qg6 9 Nb5 with more than enough compensation). And if **6...Nf6 7 Qb3, Nd8 8 Nbd2, g6 9 dxe5** White has the usual advantage in space (Levenfish-Tolush, Leningrad 1939).

Black can also return the game to a Hungarian Defense with **4...Be7** but that requires some king side disruption after **5 Qb3, Nh6 6 d4, 0-0!? 7 Bxh6, gxh6.** In Makarichev-Averbakh, Moscow Championship, White continued **8 Nbd2, Na5 9 Qc2, Nxc4 10 Nxc4, f5 11 Ne3, fxe4 12 Qxe4, exd4 13 cxd4, c6 14 0-0, d5 15 Qd3, Bd6** but he can do better with **13 Nxd4** followed by a subsequent **Nf5.**

5 d4 g6

We are now approximating the Black policy in the Strong Point Variation (chapter five) except that Black's bishop will be on g7 rather than b6.

6 0-0

A simple approach. White can also go for the jugular with **6 dxe5, dxe5 7 Ng5, Nh6 8 h4!?,** following analysis by Gufeld that runs: **8...f6 9 Nf3, Bg4 10 Qb3, Rb8 11 Nbd2** with unclear chances. We prefer the solid approach.

6 ... Bg7

7 dxe5

There is something to be said for the quiet policy of **7 Re1, Nf6 8 Bb3, 0-0 9 h3** as in Chapter Five (e.g. 9...Bd7 10 Nbd2, Rae8 11 Nf1, Qd8 12 Ng3, Qc8 13 Qd3, a6 14 Bg5, h6 15 Be3, Kh7 16 Rad1, Gorelov-Bakulin, Moscow 1981). The point of the text exchange is to exploit the slight development gap created by Black's fourth and fifth moves.

7 ... Nxe5

Black generally wants an exchange of at least one pair of minor pieces, as his game is freed compared with **7...dxe5 8 Be3, Nf6 9 Nbd2, 0-0 10 b4**.

8 Nxe5 Qxe5?!

Inconsistent with the spirit of this line — as well as risky. White could answer **8...dxe5** as above with Be3 and b2-b4.

9 Be3

And with **10 Bd4** White will have a slight edge as in Gipslis-Vorotnikov, Tbilisi 1979. See illustrative game number **24.**

(c)

3...g6
(after 1 e4, e5 2 Nf3, Nc6 3 Bc4)

4 d4 ...

Since Black has not developed anything at move three he is more vulnerable to this assault in the center (e.g. 4...d6? 5 dxe5, dxe5 6 Qxd8 ch costs a pawn). After **4 c3** Black can use the extra tempo to reach an Alekhine-Variation position with **4...d6 5 d4, Qe7**. See illustrative game 25.

4 ... exd4

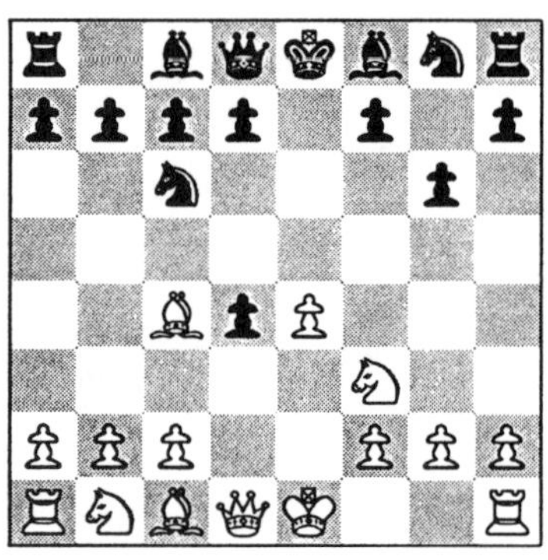

5 Bg5

Most books recommend the gambit line **5 c3**, based on Wolfgang Unzicker's analysis which runs **5...dxc3 6 Nxc3, Bg7?** (6...d6!) **7 Qb3, Qe7 8 Nd5, Qxe4 ch 9 Be2** and Black has major problems completing his development —

9...Kd8 10 0-0!, Qxe2 11 Bg5 ch, f6 12 Rfe1.

The merit of **5 Bg5** is that it reaches a favorable position without risk.

5 ... Be7

This position can be compared with Steinitz's fianchetto defense to the Ruy Lopez (1 e4, e5 2 Nf3, Nc6 3 Bb5, g6 4 d4, exd4 5 Bg5). It is safe to assume White's bishop is better placed on c4 than on b5, as in the Lopez. This becomes clear after **5...f6 6 Bf4** when White prevents Black from castling.

One of the few games that got that far (Wettering-Beisser, Correspondence 1972) continued **6...Bg7 7 Nxd4, Nge7 8 Nc3, Nxd4 9 Qxd4, d6 10 0-0-0** and White soon had an overwhelming superiority in the center (10...Bd7 11 Rhe1, Qc8 12 Qe3, Be6 13 Nd5, Kf7 14 Nxc7!).

6 Bxe7

Also possible is **6 Bf4** or **6 h4**, but then Black gets some play from **6...Nf6 7 e5, Nh5.**

6 ... Qxe7
7 0-0

(See diagram, next page)

The exchange of bishops leaves Black's king side a bit more vulnerable than usual and the e-pawn remains untakeable (7...Nf6 8 Re1, Nxe4? 9 Bb5).

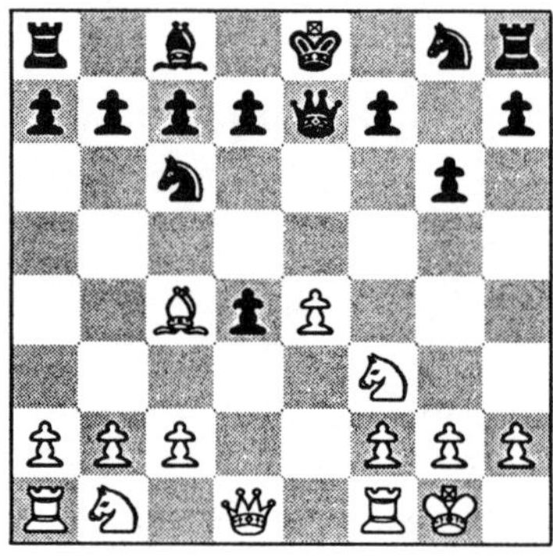

(Position after 7 0-0)

(d)

3...Qf6?
(after 1 e4, e5 2 Nf3, Nc6 3 Bc4)

This move, although discouraging **4 d4**, is just asking for trouble.

4 Nc3 Nge7

Black cannot allow **5 Nd5** cleanly.

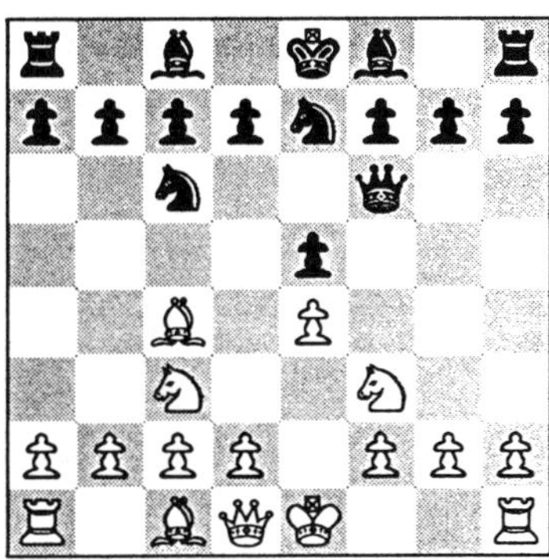

Black has stopped d2-d4 and discouraged Nd5 but his queen is misplaced and his c7 is vulnerable.

5 Nb5! Kd8
6 d4

This follows another Unzicker analysis which continues **6...exd4 7 Bg5, Qg6 8 0-0, f6 9 Bf4, d6 10 Nbxd4, Qxe4** and ends up in White's favor following **11 Qd2** and **Rfe1**.

(e)

3...f5
(after 1 e4, e5 2 Nf3, Nc6 3 Bc4)

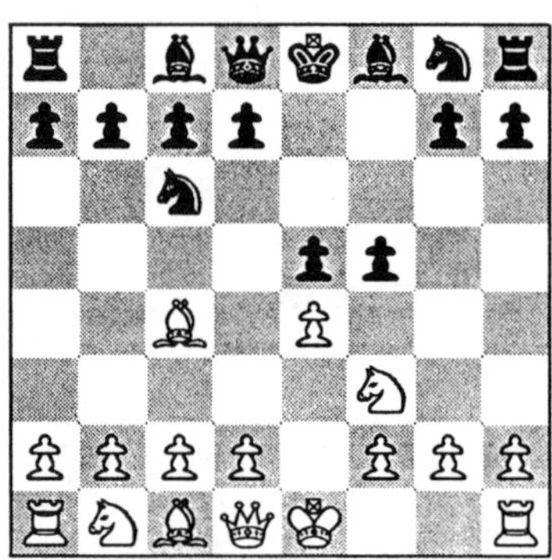

Unlike the Schliemann Defense to the Lopez, when White's bishop rests on b5, this is too risky here. Black is, in fact, transposing into an inferior version of the Latvian (1 e4, e5 2 Nf3, f5).

4 d4!

As usual, this is a strong move here. Now **4...Nf6 5 dxe5, Nxe4** leaves Black with serious problems of completing his development with ...0-0. An old German analysis runs **6 0-0, Bc5 7 Nc3, Nxc3 8 bxc3, h6 9 Nd4, g6 10 Nb3.**

4 ... d6

Not an attractive move but there were none. After **4...fxe4 5 Nxe5, d5** White's bishop is kicked from one good diagonal to another — **6 Bb5, Nge7 7 0-0, a6 8 Bxc6 ch, Nxc6 9 Qh5 ch** or **8...bxc6 9 h3** with advantage.

5 dxe5! dxe5

On **5...fxe4**, the move Black wanted to play at move four or five, White responds **6 Qd5!**, hitting at f7 and e4 and winning at least a pawn.

6 Qxd8 ch

The endgame is bad for Black on **6...Kxd8 7 Bg5 ch, Nf6 8 Nc3** or, as in a Morphy game, **6...Nxd8 7 Nxe5, fxe4 8 Bd2, Bd6 9 Bc3**.

(f)

3...Nd4
(after 1 e4, e5 2 Nf3, Nc6 3 Bc4)

And here, unlike the comparable position from the Bird Defense of the Ruy Lopez, this knight move threatens nothing. Its chief, and perhaps only virtue, is to set up the 16th century trap of **4 Nxe5??, Qg5 5 Nxf7, Qxg2 6 Rf1, Qxe4 ch** and wins.

4 c3!

Of course, White gets at least a small edge now.

4	**...**	**Nxf3 ch**
5	**Qxf3**	**Qf6**

No better is **5...Nf6 6 d4, d6 7 Bg5**, as suggested by the Soviet analyst Neishtadt.

6 Qg3

And White, with **7 0-0** and **8 f4** in view, retains an initiative.

Illustrative games:

(25) Vasiukov-Gildardo Garcia, Cienfuegos 1975 —
1 e4, e5 2 Nf3, Nc6 3 Bc4, Be7 4 d4, d6 5 dxe5, dxe5 6 Qxd8 ch, Bxd8 7 Nc3, Nf6 8 Be3, Nd7 9 0-0-0, Nb6 10 Bb5, f6 11 a4! (The beginning of a queen side attack. Now 11...a5 12 Nd5 or 11...a6 12 Bxc6 ch, bxc6 13 a5 gains space for White.) **Bd7 12 a5, Nc8 13 a6!,**

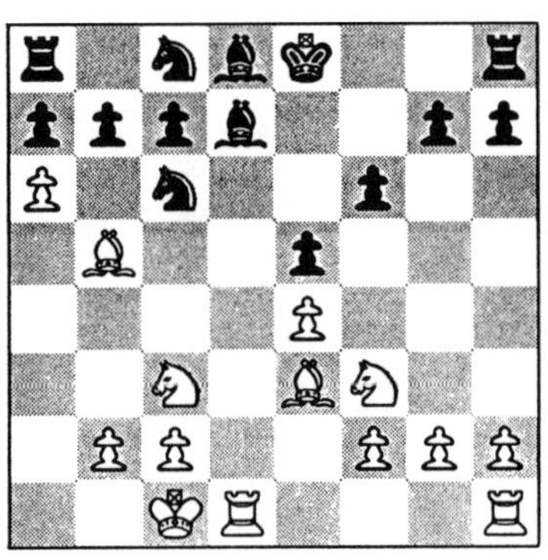

13...Nd6 14 axb7, Rb8 15 Ba4, Rxb7 16 Bc5, Be7 17 Nd5, Na5 18 Bxd7 ch, Kxd7 19 Nd2, Rd8 20 Rhe1, Ke8 21 f4, Nc6 22 fxe5, Nxe5 23 Nf3, Nc8 24 Nxe5, fxe5 25 Bxe7, Nxe7 26 c3 (Now on 26...Nxd5? 27 exd5, Black's pawns are split into four islands and begin to fall.), **Nc8 27 Kc2, Nd6 28 Nb4, Nf7 29 Rxd8 ch, Kxd8 30 Rd1 ch, Ke7 31 Rd5, Ke6 32 Na6!, c6 33 Nc5 ch, Ke7 34 Nxb7, cxd5 35 exd5, e4 36 c4, Ne5 37 Kc3, e3 38 b3, g5 39 Nc5, a5 40 h3, h5** and **Black resigned.**

(26) Gipslis-Vorotnikov, Tbilisi 1979 —
1 e4, e5 2 Nf3, Nc6 3 Bc4, d6 4 c3, Qe7 5 d4,

g6 6 0-0, Bg7 7 dxe5, Nxe5 8 Nxe5, Qxe5 9 Be3, Nf6 10 Bd4, Qh5 11 f3!, 0-0 12 Nd2, Bd7 13 Re1, Bc6 14 Nf1, Qg5 15 Ne3, Nh5 16 Ng4, Nf4 17 g3, Bxd4 ch 18 Qxd4, Ne6 19 Bxe6!, fxe6

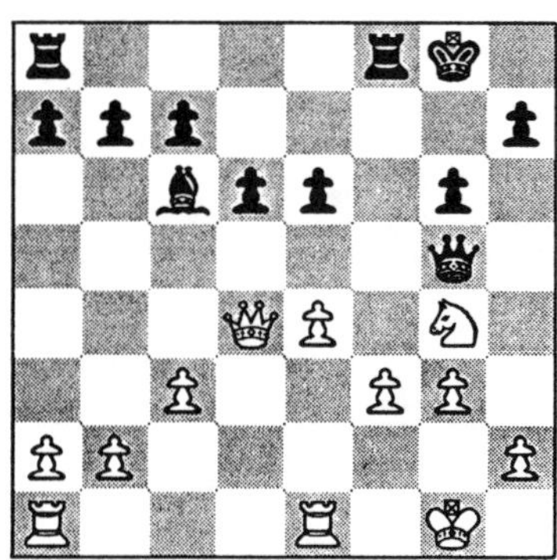

20 h4, (Wins material because of 20...Qe7?? 21 Nh6 mate.) **Qh5 21 Nf6 ch, Rxf6 22 Qxf6, Rf8 23 Qxe6 ch, Kg7 24 Qg4, Qb5 25 Rf1, Qxb2 26 Rac1, Qxa2 27 Rf2, Qa5 28 Qg5, Qxg5 29 hxg5, Re8 30 Ra2, d5 31 exd5, Bxd5 32 Rd2, Bc6 33 Kf2, h6 34 gxh6 ch, Kxh6 35 Re2, Rd8 36 Re7, Rd3 37 Rf7, g5 38 Ke2, Rd6 39 Rh1 ch, Kg6 40 R1h7, Re6 41 Kf2, Rd6 42 Rhg7 ch, Kh6 43 g4, a5 44 Rxc7, Rd3 45 Rge7!, Rd6 46 c4 Resigns**

(27) Mednis-Korchnoi, Vienna 1986 —

1 e4, e5 2 Nf3, Nc6 3 Bc4, g6 4 c3, d6 5 d4, Qe7 6 dxe5?!, Nxe5! (After this exchange of minor pieces, White should only have a slight advantage.) **7 Nxe5, dxe5 8 0-0, Nf6 9 Qf3, Be6 10 Bg5, Bg7 11 Nd2, h6** (Mednis says 11...0-0! equalizes.) **12 Bxf6, Bxf6 13 Bxe6, Qxe6**

14 Nc4, Bg5?! (Trying to sharpen the position rather than play for equality with 14...Qxc4! 15 Qxf6, 0-0 16 Qxe5, Rfe8!) **15 b3, 0-0-0 16 Rad1, c6 17 Rxd8 ch, Rxd8 18 Rd1, h5 19 Rxd8 ch, Bxd8??** (A simple oversight. Black should not fear 19...Kxd8 20 Qg3, Bf4 21 Qd3, Kc7 22 g3, as shown by Mednis.)

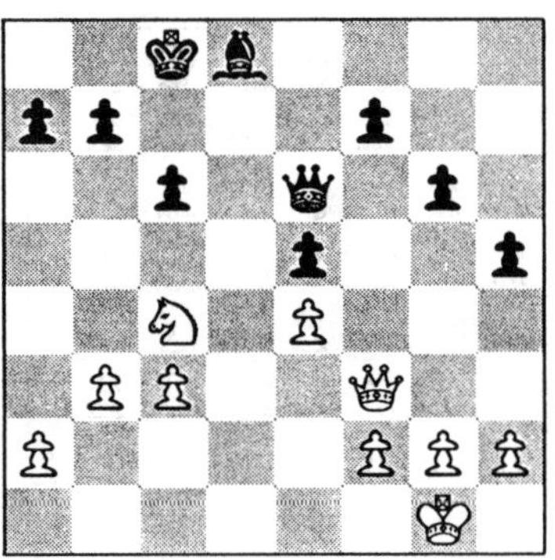

20 Qxf7! (Wins a pawn because of the knight fork.), **Qxf7 21 Nd6 ch, Kc7 22 Nxf7, Bf6 23 Kf1, Resigns.**

NOTES

NOTES

NOTES

NOTES